Fishing In Oregon's

ENDLESS SEASON

Also by Scott Richmond

Fishing In Oregon's Cascade Lakes
Fishing in Oregon's Deschutes River
The Pocket Gillie

Fishing in Oregon's
ENDLESS SEASON

Scott Richmond

Drawings by Guy Jacobson

Flying Pencil Publications
Scappoose, Oregon

Published by Flying Pencil Publications in collaboration with Four Rivers Press. Address all inquiries to:
    Flying Pencil Publications
    33126 SW Callahan Road
    Scappoose, Oregon 97056
    (503) 543-7171

Narrative drawings by Guy Jacobson. Technical illustrations by Lora Creswick and Kari Valley. Maps by Madelynne Sheehan. Cover art by Vic Ericson. Cover design by John Laursen.

Printed in the United States of America.

10 9 8 7 6 5 4 3 2 1

Library of Congress Catalog Card Number: 96-086821

ISBN: 0-916473-11-2

Acknowledgements

Maddy Sheehan for editing and encouragement. Jim Manual for review of text and many useful suggestions. Nick Verlotta for salmon fishing advice. John DeFore, Don Schwartz, and Frank Amato for sturgeon background. Jeff Harris and John Wair for technical assistance. Dave Hughes, Pat Wray, Bill Kremers, Mark Bachman, Martin James, Jim Dexter, and all the others I encountered along the way; you're welcome at my campfire anytime. John Laursen for cover design and book design consultation, Guy Jacobson for drawings, Vic Ericson for cover art, Kari Valley and Lora Creswick for technical illustrations, Myra Clark for layout consultation.

Contents

Maps

Illustrations

Waters Fished
During the Endless Season

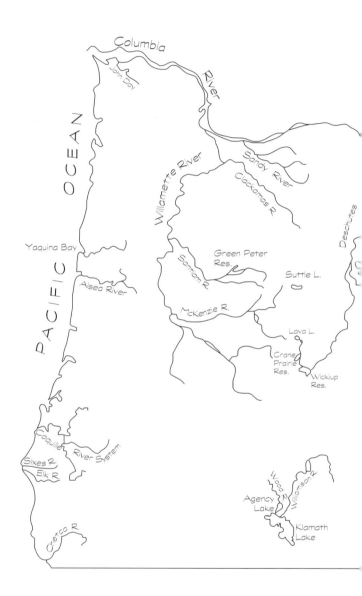

John Day River

River

River

Owyhee R

○ Chickahominy
Reservoir

Preface

The beauty of Oregon's fishing is its diversity. In every season, from environments as different as rainforest and desert, mountain and estuary, seductive voices rise from rivers, lakes, creeks, ponds, sloughs, bays, and ocean: *try me, try me,* they say.

Fishing in Oregon's Endless Season is a collection of essays drawn from a 53-week span when I heeded those voices as much as time, work, and the long-suffering patience of my family permitted. For a year plus a week I pursued 17 species of fish in over 25 Oregon rivers and lakes.

Nevertheless, I didn't even come close to covering the full range of Oregon's fishing opportunities. There were trips I planned but didn't take, rivers close to my heart in which I never wet a line, fish I wanted to catch but couldn't find time for.

Despite these omissions, I hope those new to Oregon will find this book to be a practical introduction to the excellent fishing that lies within their reach every day of the year. I hope those who have lived here awhile will read this book and feel inspired to branch out to new fisheries. And I hope those fortunate anglers who have spent a lifetime fishing the state's waters will read about familiar places and smile with fond recognition.

But most of all, I hope that everyone who reads *Fishing in Oregon's Endless Season* will recognize the great gift the Oregon Country offers to anglers. Enjoy that gift, embrace it with all your soul, and take care of it so anglers not yet born can know what we have shared.

Scott Richmond
West Linn, Oregon
October 1996

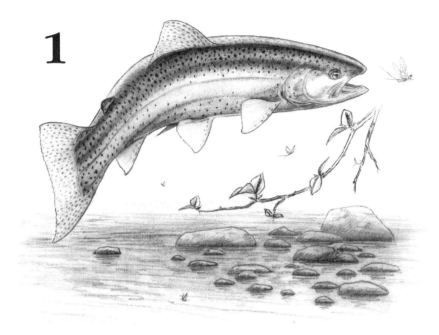

1

March Brown

Early March, McKenzie River below Hayden Bridge

On this cool but cloudless day in early March, the banks of the McKenzie River were a mare's nest of vines and twigs backed by a jumble of firs, alders, and cottonwoods. All but the firs were leafless. Maddy Sheehan propped her wader-clad feet on the gunnel of my anchored driftboat, leaned back in her seat, and munched a tunafish sandwich. An oiled Filson hat was tipped back on her head, and a purple neck scarf warded off the March wind.

During our riverside lunch, Maddy and I exchanged impressions of some of Oregon's lesser-known angling hot spots. She is the author of *Fishing in Oregon*, guidebook to all the state's fishing, so when she talks, I listen. Although the conversation was in earnest, neither of us made eye contact because we were searching the river for rises.

"Have you been up the Wenaha in the Wenaha-Tucanon Wilderness?" Maddy was saying. "If you're fishing the Grande Ronde, you ought to. . ."

I almost choked on the apple I was eating—not in anticipation of fishing the Wenaha, but because I'd just seen a March brown mayfly floating the McKenzie. I croaked, "There's one!"

Maddy squinted in the direction indicated by my finger. As we watched, a bulls-eye of ripples appeared, and a trout inhaled the mayfly.

"Yes." I said, my voice returning to normal. "Yes!"

It was the bare bones world of late winter, a skeletal landscape painted with a narrow brush and a muted palette. But there were signs that the season would soon yield to spring: a few alders had a green tint; an osprey, recently returned from its equatorial migration, perched on a snag; the wind was cool, but not as bitter as last month.

And I'd just seen my first March brown of the year.

For the last three months, my fishing had consisted of either dredging rivers with big lures in search of winter-run steelhead, or casting tiny dry flies to fussy trout in desert streams. While those are enjoyable pursuits, they are about the only winter fishing options in Oregon, and I was beginning to chafe under the constraints. Now that was about to change.

The March brown is the first big bug of the year, and when the McKenzie's trout sip the duns, it heralds the awakening of opportunities that have lain dormant for months. Spring salmon, lake fishing, the salmonfly hatch, bass, and a host of other angling pursuits follow in the wake of that first rise to a March brown. It's the time of maximum anticipation of all that will follow.

I'd call it the start of the fishing season, but in Oregon *fishing season* is a meaningless phrase. Oh, there are times when certain

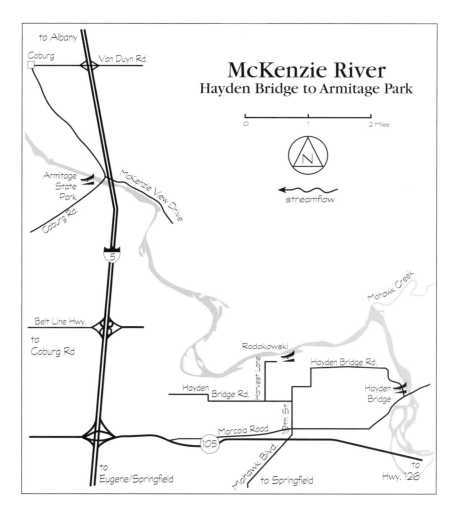

McKenzie River

Hayden Bridge to Armitage Park

rivers and lakes are closed, and months when some species are not available, but Oregon is blessed with such a wide range of environments—saltwater, coastal creeks, valley rivers, mountain lakes, desert streams and reservoirs—that something good is always happening somewhere, though it never happens the same way two years running.

While the opportunities tend to be cyclical, they are far from predictable. For example, I know that every afternoon in late winter the McKenzie's March browns will hatch at around 1:30. But the strength of the hatch and the trout's reaction to it depends on the weather and river levels, and probably a dozen other factors even less understood than the first two. In fact, events that happened more than a year ago can directly affect today's fishing.

Oregon's angling is like its weather: predictable only in a general sense and full of the unexpected. I suppose there is some place in the world where the fishing is as regular and reliable as a Swiss clock. I hope I never go there.

The apple was exchanged for a fly rod, and I climbed out of the driftboat into knee-deep water. I waded upstream and began casting a size 12 Comparadun to a featureless run. Maddy was throwing the same pattern about 100 feet below me.

At the beginning of a hatch, the whole world narrows to the river, and nothing exists but anticipation. I waited for a crescendo of activity, with duns sprinkled from bank to bank and eager trout dimpling the river. It never happened. Maddy caught a pair of 12-inch cutthroat, then I had one, but half an hour after the first dun appeared on the river, the hatch petered out. That's typical. Some days the March brown hatch is heavy, but other times it's like today: a sputtering event that never gathers momentum.

Upstream, a submerged boulder split the current into two braids, and trout rose in each, although there were few rises elsewhere in the river. I whistled to Maddy and waved her to the boat. We climbed in, and I rowed against the current until we were just below and to one side of the boulder.

We cast to where the trout rose and watched intently as our Comparaduns drifted through the feeding lane. The fish ignored them. Seconds after our flies passed over the trout, they rose again. Two hundred feet away, at the beginning of the hatch, a few fish had accepted our Comparaduns. Now, with even more trout rising, the same fly was ignored.

I peered at the water and saw what should have been obvious from the moment we dropped anchor. "Caddis," I said, as if that answered all the world's questions. This was a completely different kind of insect and required a different fly.

Maddy had also taken a close look at the bugs drifting past. "They're coming from above," she said. "They're not hatching."

I took another squint at the river, then the air above it. Maddy was right. "They're laying eggs," I said.

"Do you think an Elk Hair would work?"

"Should work," I said. "But. . ." I shrugged.

We each tied on an Elk Hair Caddis and cast again. The trout had no more interest in them than in the Comparaduns.

I opened a fly box and stared at it like it was the Delphic Oracle, then poked around in the caddis bins. I pulled out a small, gray-bodied fly—the only one of its kind in my box—and tied it on.

The first cast had drifted about three feet when a trout rose and confidently sucked it down. "Ha!" I exulted. There is no elation like knowing you've found the right fly. I pulled the fish to the boat and held the leader in my left hand while I tried to take the trout's picture. It flopped, then rolled, then pulled hard and was gone. My fly—the perfect fly, the right fly for the moment, the only fly of its kind that either of us possessed—was still hooked in its jaw.

I carry at least three boxes of flies for river fishing, but no matter how many flies I put in them, there are several times a year when I run out of the only one the fish want. When this happens, I go home, tie up a dozen of the magic fly, and put them in the box. Usually, they never work again.

I rummaged through my fly boxes some more, then tied on a small Adams, the world's most generic dry fly. On the next cast, a trout rose and took it. Maddy switched to an Adams and soon hooked a fish, too. As long as we cast to the current seam and the fly drifted without drag, a trout would rise to take it.

After a few more cutthroat, I put my rod down and just watched. The trout lay in about three feet of clear water, but their dark green backs camouflaged them so well that they were invisible until they rose to take a caddis from the surface. First there was a shadowy hint of movement, then a dark shape took form, and finally a silver-sided cutthroat would be clearly seen. A mouth would open, the fly would disappear, and Maddy's rod would bend again.

March Browns

The western March brown mayfly is a member of the genus Rhithrogena. *The nymphs live almost a year in the river and hatch into adults beginning in early March. Daily hatches can continue into April. Emergence is usually between 1:00 and 2:00 in the afternoon and only lasts an hour or two, at most. The best hatches occur on cool, drizzly days; if you're not suffering, you're not going to have good fishing.*

March browns are part of the "clinger" group of mayflies, which means the nymphs are streamlined and well-adapted to life in fast, riffly water. It also means the nymphs are seldom knocked lose in the current, so they are rarely eaten by trout until they begin hatching.

Like most members of the clinger group, March browns emerge ambiguously. Usually the nymphs pop to the surface and the dun hatches out and drifts on the current. In this case, a dry fly is the best choice. But sometimes emergence takes place underwater and the dun rises to the surface. When this happens, the answer is a wet fly, such as a Soft Hackle.

It can be tough to tell whether you're facing a surface or an underwater emergence, and if you don't get it right you won't have many fish. Despite what the books and magazines say, you can't always know what's happening by looking at the rise forms of the trout. So start with a dry fly such as a Comparadun, but if that doesn't work, tie on a brown Soft Hackle, size 12 or 14.

March brown hatches are excellent on many rivers in the Willamette Valley, such as the McKenzie and mainstem Willamette near Eugene. I've also seen outstanding hatches on the Rogue. The middle Deschutes near Terrebonne is another good March brown river, but I feel the hatch there tends to be about two weeks later than on the Valley rivers.

The caddis faded after about 45 minutes, and the trout settled back to the bottom and refused to be budged. I up-anchored, and we continued our drift. The best part of the fishing was over; it always ends too soon in March. We had hopes for a few stragglers, though, and cast as we drifted.

This part of the river skirts the city of Springfield, offering a mix of the wild and the domestic. On one bank I spied a young beaver, while on the opposite side a large suburban home sprawled across a manicured lawn. I heard a woodpecker hammer at a snag, then the babble of schoolchildren at recess. The cry of a hawk was followed by a whistle at the lumber mill.

One of the pleasures I take from drifting the McKenzie is that it's the ancestral home of my driftboat. This style of rivercraft evolved here and on the Rogue River. After a Darwinian process that included many half-drowned oarsmen and a few cords of splintered wood, the boats took on today's river-worthy shape. Now most are made of aluminum and fiberglass, though there are still a few being built of wood. In other parts of the country they are known as McKenzie boats, but in Oregon they are as common as raindrops and are simply called driftboats.

As we floated, Maddy told me how her two girls were doing (one in her first year at the University of Oregon, the other nearing the end of high school), and I updated her on my two daughters (one a high school sophomore, the other a junior in college). Talk of family and business mingled with casting for trout. Maddy hooked a few more fish, including a nice 15-inch wild rainbow, and I picked up another cutthroat. All too soon we arrived at the Rodakowski takeout.

On the drive home, I thought about the day's fishing. The March browns had made their appearance, and that always gets me pumped and feeling like another angling year has begun. But the hatch had quickly fizzled, and the trout were taking egg-laying caddis. The best fly was an Adams, which is really more of a mayfly imitation and only remotely resembles a caddisfly.

Were these shifts and ambiguities an omen of the coming months? Unquestionably so—since that's the way fishing is in Oregon. Each trip is like a green-backed trout in deep water, invisible against the backdrop of river and stone until it rises, takes shape, and reveals its true nature. The March brown hatch that turned into a caddis show was just a reminder that my fishing year would include the usual mixture of frustrations and elations, failures and triumphs—that I should expect the unexpected, remain flexible, and never rule out any possible solution to an angling dilemma. And it would matter little how often my rod bent because with fishing, as with many things in life, the real purpose is not the catch, but the quest.

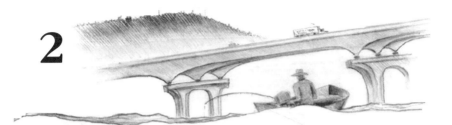

2

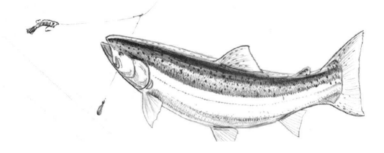

Whose Fish?

Willamette River near Oregon City

Have you heard how professional gamblers let an easy mark win a few hands, then once he's suckered into the game, they scam him for all he's got? Rivers can be like that.

On my first salmon fishing trip to the Willamette, I went with someone who knew what he was doing. Under his guidance, I landed a 28-pound spring chinook. Inspired by this easy success, I returned to the river on my own the following spring.

Before heading for the boat ramp, I hosed out my skiff, a 14-foot Klamath, then ran the 8-horse outboard for a few minutes, just to make sure it was OK. It sounded rough, but I was sure that once it was warmed up it would purr like a cat by the fire.

I drove to Clackamette Park at Oregon City, slid the boat off the trailer, and beached it. When I returned from parking the car, the boat looked a bit odd, kind of down at the stern. My shoulders sagged as I realized I'd forgotten to reseat the drain plug. When I reached the boat, it was half full of water.

Fortunately, I'd worn my chest waders (they make good rain pants and it was a drippy day) and could walk around the boat in the water while I bailed it out. Unfortunately, the waders leaked and cold water poured in around my left ankle.

Once the boat was bailed, I set forth on the river. My cold left leg made me shiver, but that was nothing compared to the way the motor was shaking. It was running unevenly, as if only one cylinder was firing. I figured it would soon clear up, and I motored down the Clackamas. At its confluence with the Willamette, a hog line—a line of boats anchored rail to rail—stretched across the river. Fishing lines streamed behind every boat, and the remaining space was filled by the casts of bank anglers. Getting to the Willamette would be like passing through one of those bead curtains that sometimes hang in doorways. Anglers glowered at me as I squeezed through. I kept my head down and fiddled with my fish locator, a device whose batteries I soon realized were as dead as a fossil.

I pointed the boat upstream and opened the throttle to full power. Brown water rushed past me, and the shore sped by. Unfortunately, the shore was speeding in the wrong direction. My motor wheezed and sputtered but could make no headway against the current. I was being swept downstream.

My mind filled with back-up plans: if I couldn't get back to Clackamette Park, how far was it to the next downstream boat ramp, and how could I get my car and trailer to it? The current was slower near the shore, though, and I found that by edging close to the bank I could creep back to the Clackamas. This brought me face-to-face with the hog line. I smiled tightly and avoided eye-contact as I passed once more through the monofilament curtain and crawled upriver like a whipped puppy. When I finally reached the boat ramp, I had a raging headache. I skipped the salmon for the rest of that spring.

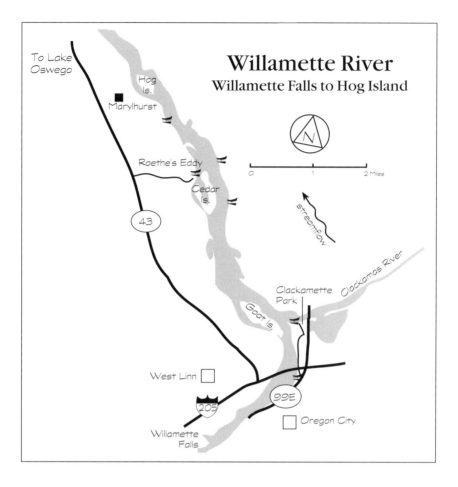

Willamette River

Willamette Falls to Hog Island

This year—one year after the drainplug fiasco—I was ready to launch my boat for another spring fling with Willamette chinook. I went to the Cedar Oaks boat ramp, a launching point that avoided hog lines. I checked the boat before sliding it into the river: drain plug secure, fresh batteries in the locator, motor fresh from a spring tune-up, leak-proof pants. Now if I just knew what I was doing, I might catch a salmon.

Lack of knowledge was the key issue. When I was growing up, my father and I spent a lot of time on Puget Sound chasing salmon, but everything I knew about salmon fishing was of little use to me on a river.

I have a standard approach to new fishing experiences like this. First, I go out and poke around with no expectation of catching fish, or even of wetting a line—just see where people are fishing and how they're going about it. I'd done this a couple of days before, then took step two: learn from the experience of others. I went to a free seminar at a fishing store. On the way out, I picked up some one-page "how-to-do-it" flyers they had near the check-out stand. Neither the seminar nor the flyers were very detailed, so I called an acquaintance who knew what he was doing and invited him to lunch. Over sandwiches and coffee he filled in a few blanks and answered questions.

When starting something new, it's easy to be confused. Sought and unsought advice comes from several sources. Often these "experts" don't agree, and a neophyte can be dazed by conflicting opinions. Bait or lure? If bait, which one and rigged how? Troll or still fish? If trolling, how fast, where, and how deep? If anchored, where?

I try to narrow my focus to a few basic issues. I feel there are only four questions I need to answer in order to catch fish:

What kind of lure or bait should I present to the fish?

Where should I present it?

How should I present it?

When should I present it?

From talking to people with experience, I learned that trolling worked as well as anything for the Willamette's chinook, and prawns were an effective bait. I also found that plenty of salmon were caught between Cedar Oaks Park and the falls at Oregon City. Fish could be caught at any time of day, but dawn through early afternoon were the best times, and April and May were the best months. This answered the questions of what, where, how, and when. There were other places I could go and other ways to fish, but I had a basic approach that was good enough. I would stick to it like a bulldog until I mastered it.

The Willamette spring chinook fishery is an urban experience. The river flows through the middle of downtown Portland, and there's some good fishing there. My stalking ground was a few miles up-stream, so I saw more houses than skyscrapers. Even while sur-rounded by humanity, however, you still know you're on a river. Herons, geese, ducks, and kingfishers are common, and beaver and otter can be spotted if you look carefully.

April is a particularly nice month to be on the Willamette. Canada geese frequent the river, and I've often seen a goose and a gander paddling the margins with a brood of goslings between them. They always remind me of a small-town family out for a Sunday stroll.

The Willamette offers a multitude of rewarding sights, most of which don't fit in a salmon net, but I find it takes conscious effort to slow down when I'm fishing here, to focus less on my rod and more on what's around me. The drawback of an urban fishery is the ten-dency to pack citified intensity into your tackle bag

My first four trips to the Willamette were half-day affairs where my goal was not fish, but more knowledge. Of course, a salmon would have been nice, too, but it didn't happen. I found a couple of good places to troll: Roethe's Eddy, which was just in front of the boat ramp; and the area alongside and downstream from Goat Island (sometimes called Yucca Island). I observed people who looked like they knew what they were doing and matched my trolling speed to theirs. I figured out how to rig my bait so it would roll slow-ly at trolling speed. (My goal was a five-second prawn: it would take five seconds to make a complete roll.) I like a little extra scent on my prawns, so I smarmed anchovy butter on them. A bait injector with shrimp oil probably would have worked just as well.

Adding fish-attracting scent is important, but it's even more im-portant to subtract fish-repelling odors such as human scent, gaso-line, and sunscreen. I've been told by people who know these things that dogs have a sense of smell 100 times better than a human's, and a grizzly bear's nose is 100 times better than a dog's. A salmon's sense of smell is 100 times keener than a grizzly's.

This means a salmon's schnoz is a million times more sensitive

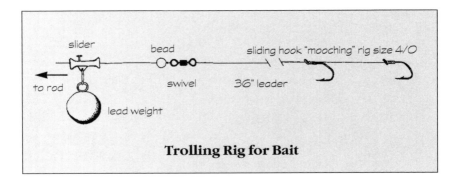

Trolling Rig for Bait

than mine. I think about that every time I use bait, so I always carry a soap that removes human scent and other odors. I won't even touch my bait until I've washed my hands, nor will I put my bait on anything that might carry odor, such as the bottom of the boat, which is always going to smell like gasoline.

I should say here that I seldom use bait. The problem is, I can't constrain the odor to my terminal gear. I get it on my hands, my pants, my shirt, my boat—everywhere. I make it worse by propping my chin in my palm when I troll. I have a beard, so the strong smell of bait is transferred from hand to whiskers, and I come home with a face smelling of anchovy and prawns. My wife, Barbara, won't come within ten feet of me. "Go away!" she says. "Kissing you is like smooching a can of sardines." On the other hand, the cats think I'm finger-licking good.

My fifth morning on the Willamette, I was prowling Roethe's Eddy along with several other boats. It was a lovely day, with blue sky and mild temperatures. The river was not too high and was running a nice green color.

One of the boats in the eddy was a Sea Nymph with a lone angler. He was watching his rod carefully and gave it a little twitch. Suddenly, it bent deeply and he was onto a salmon. I trolled past him after he netted it. "Nice fish," I said. "About 20 pounds?"

"More like 17," he said. "Took my bait weird. Just pecked at it like a squawfish, so I jerked the bait away. When I yanked, all hell broke lose." He held the fish up, a bright female. "It took my bait in 18 feet of water," he said. "When the river's clear like this, I catch all my fish on the bottom where it's 18-feet deep. When it's murky, I catch them at six to ten feet."

He looked like he knew what he doing, so I paid attention. After that, I watched the depth carefully on my fish finder and trolled along the 18-foot contour line. The first thing I noticed was that most of the hog lines were positioned so the anglers' baits were at places where the bottom shelved to 18 feet. The other thing I noticed was that most other trollers were following the same line.

This was not a good year for Willamette salmon. Returns were low compared to previous runs, and there were many anglers chasing a small number of chinook. It appeared that on any day, one out of ten rods would pick up a salmon—not the best odds. But I was feeling more confident with each trip. If I kept doing the right things in the right places, I would eventually connect with a salmon, and when I saw someone else catch a fish I figured it could have been me. Com-pulsive gamblers probably have similar thoughts.

When many people are pursuing a small number of fish in the same place and in the same way, who catches the fish can seem like a question of converging probabilities, also known as dumb luck. It works like this: you troll past a prime spot; two minutes later another angler goes past the same place, only now a willing fish has moved into it and bingo, the other angler catches the salmon. If you'd been there, you'd have caught it.

This gives rise to envy. Everyone feels that salmon was theirs. I know I felt that way when the guy in the Sea Nymph landed his fish. I'd trolled through the same water several times that morning. So had he. When the salmon moved in, his boat was in the right place at the right time, and mine wasn't. But I couldn't help feeling he'd caught my fish. I'm sure if I had hooked it, he'd have felt the same way.

The next day, I fished Roethe's Eddy a little, but nobody was catching anything there. I went upstream near Goat Island and passed a hog line at the downstream end of the trolling area. Some anglers in the hog line were reading the newspaper, others chatted with neighbors. I thought I heard a telephone ring, and an angler pulled out a cellular phone and began talking.

Hog lines have a communal nature, like a neighborhood cafe. Often the same people show up in the same hog lines day after day, and a camaraderie develops. But they're not for me. I need to feel like I'm *doing* something, and the wait-for-something-to-come-along nature of hog lines is not my style. The average age of hog-liners is noticeably higher than that of trollers, so maybe when I'm older they'll have more appeal.

In the hog line, I saw a relaxed-looking man in a blue cap sipping coffee from a metal cup. Suddenly he sat upright, alert and watching his rod like a cat watches a mouse. Then he pounced, jerked the rod, and was onto a fish. Others in the hog line shouted encouragement as he held the rod in one hand and uncleated his anchorline with the other. He played the fish as he drifted downstream, his anchorline marked by a buoy.

I saw him return to the hog line 10 minutes later. He held up a typical fish, about 15 pounds, and murmurs of congratulations could be heard. But I knew every angler in that hog line was thinking the same thing: It should have been me. It was *my* fish.

I continued to troll. There was a pull on my line, a quick, hard pluck. There was no hookup, so I released line from the reel (I'd been told this was what I should do). Nothing happened, though, so I reeled up. The head of my prawn was gone. I'd definitely had a bite, my first in five trips. As I rigged a fresh prawn, I contemplated the legs dangling behind it. They looked like something a fish could pull on and miss the hooks. From then on, I trimmed the legs from each of my prawns.

I had no further bites that day, but on my next trip, two days later, I had another pull. This time the whole prawn was gone. *At least*, I thought, *I'm getting closer to hooking a salmon.*

I replaced the missing prawn. The new bait had a nice slow roll, a true five-second prawn. I continued to troll, working the area downstream from Goat Island. I had lots of company. Boats would head upstream along one line—the best line, I thought—then come downstream farther from shore but as close as possible to the prime area.

I was headed upstream, rod under my arm and pointing toward mid-river. A 20-foot aluminum boat passed me going the other way. Suddenly, my rod bounced once, then bounced again and dove for the water. It bent double, and line ripped off the reel as the salmon raced for mid-river.

"Fish on!" I yelled at the boat that had just passed me. "Watch your lines!" The salmon came to the surface, and I had a brief glimpse of its bright, slab sides. It was a big fish, 20 pounds easy, 25 probably, 30 maybe.

The fish's path was straight across the lines trailing from the other boat. A grizzled angler looked startled, then grabbed his rod and started to reel in. My fish was now clearly fouled in his line and pulling against both rods. When someone else's fish runs into your line, you should do one of two things: either cut your line (you'll lose about $3 worth of tackle), or let your reel free-spool. Unfortunately, this angler chose to reel in, then jerked his rod a couple of times to try to free it up. Bad idea.

My line went limp, and so did I. I reeled in and saw where my leader had been sawed through. I looked at the other angler. He never glanced my way, never said, "Sorry," never even acknowledged my existence. Maybe he thought it was his fish.

I have to give him the benefit of the doubt. It happened fast, and it's hard to know how to react in a situation like that. In a crowded fishery, these things happen. At least I'd hooked a fish, but that was scant consolation. It took seven trips to the river just to get one solid grab. Would it take seven more trips before I connected again?

Three days later I returned to the river. My morning had been busy, so I didn't get there until noon. Several boats were nosing into the boat ramp as I backed the trailer. Nobody had a salmon, nor had they seen anyone else catch a salmon. It didn't look promising.

I poked around Roethe's Eddy for half an hour. It didn't feel fishy, so I motored up to Goat Island and trolled in the eddy and along the outside of the island. A white fiberglass boat, about 21 feet and holding a single fisherman, was working the same water. On the first pass, he said he'd marked a fish on his locator, and a little later I saw a guy in a hog line net a chinook. The needle on my "hope" meter went from *no way* to *slim*.

I put my rod in its holder and reached for my clipboard. I always carry a clipboard, pen, and waterproof paper so I can keep a journal of my fishing. I wrote down the date, then, "Slow day. Overcast but not raining. Saw one fish cau . . ." Out of the corner of my eye I saw my rod butt jerking back and forth. My first thought was that I'd snagged bottom, but a quick look astern revealed I'd hooked a fish.

I tossed the clipboard onto the seat, shifted the motor to neutral, and grabbed the rod. Five minutes later the salmon was near the boat and on its side. I had the net in my left hand and pulled back the rod with my right to slide the fish toward it. This is the goosiest part of fishing alone, especially when the prey is big and feisty. The lead weight can get tangled in the net, and if you miss the fish, it will break the line as it pulls away. But the salmon slid over the net, I jerked the net up, and the fish was trapped.

I felt triumphant as I lay down my rod and pulled the net into the boat. I'd forgotten to bring a club to dispatch the chinook, but the angler in the white boat loaned me his. He may or may not have figured this was his fish, but he was gracious anyway.

As I continued trolling for a couple more hours, I noticed other boats crowding me, as if I knew what I was doing. Ha!

It took me eight trips to land that salmon—not very good odds. I had four bites, two hookups, and one fish. The 8-4-2-1 progression had a neat, mathematical appeal. And there was a sense of progress: from being in the right place, to having a bite, to hooking a fish, to landing one. I figured that if present trends continued, I'd hook *two* salmon on my next trip.

The next week, however, the weather worsened and the Willamette became unfishable. I was off to the lakes in pursuit of other quarry, and never got back to the chinook. But next season—a little older, a little wiser—I'll be back playing *Whose Fish* on the Willamette.

Fishing for Spring Chinook above Willamette Falls

If the lower Willamette crowds give you hives, try the river above the Falls. The Oregon Department of Fish and Wildlife (ODFW) describes this fishery as "underutilized," which is bureaucrat-talk for "there's a lot more fish than people."

Between the Falls and the Yamhill River, the Willamette is best suited for trolling, and spinners or spoons are commonly used. Above the Yamhill, the current is stronger, and most salmon anglers anchor near the bank and let a small spinner work in the current near the bottom; use between one and two ounces of lead.

Above the Yamhill, the best water tends to be places with a rock or gravel bottom (not mud) near the bank where the water is four to six feet deep. Other good places are near current seams and drop-offs. Low-light times (dawn, dusk, overcast days) are best. The middle Willamette has sudden shoals and gravel bars. These make for good fishing, but they also require careful boating.

The San Salvador boat ramp is a popular launching point, but never leave your car parked there overnight because break-ins are common. In fact, some people will only park at places where there is frequent traffic, such as near the Wheatland Ferry.

Salmon reach this part of the river around mid-May, and fishing can be good for a month or more. The spring chinook run overlaps with the early summer steelhead run, and it is not unusual to pick up a steelhead while salmon fishing.

Casting for Memories

Early May, Eastbound

The Willamette was high and muddy, but a few anglers doggedly plied its waters for spring chinook. I was not one them. My view of the river was from above, crossing the I-205 bridge on a cold, rainy morning in early May as I headed for the lakes of central Oregon. I had three quarries in mind: trophy brown trout (from Wickiup Reservoir), trophy rainbows (Crane Prairie Reservoir), and trophy brook trout (Hosmer Lake).

Actually, *trophy* is probably not the right word since I had no plans to mount a big fish on a wall. What I really wanted was *memorable* fish, and frankly, some big fish aren't worth a second thought. I've caught more than a few lunkers that were total bores. On the other hand, some average-sized fish continue to replay in my mind, either because of their beauty, surprise, spunk, or simply the setting in which they were caught or the friends who shared my camp.

Still, big fish are by definition more unusual than average fish, and therefore more likely to create a lasting image. So I often yield to the pull of trophy-sized trout, especially in spring because that is prime time for big fish in lakes. September offers larger fare, but May's fish are hungry and aggressive as the lakes shed winter's ice. Also, it's the time of year when my own enthusiasm runs a country mile ahead of reason.

Spring weather, however, can frustrate the most ambitious plans, and I doubted I would get to fish for all three species on this trip. Big browns were the primary goal; the brooks and rainbows were alternate targets in case the browns didn't pan out. In early May, you've got to have a backup plan or three.

May is a pivot month for Oregon fishing. What happens in May can affect fishing the rest of the year, even the next several years. If the month is cool and wet, the mountain snow pack will not begin melting, and might even grow. This means the high lakes will have slow fishing until June or later. It also means irrigators will wait to draw down reservoirs or rivers, and rivers may experience a heavy run-off until late June.

On the other hand, a dry, warm May can turn on the lakes early. If this kind of May follows a winter of low snowpack, the rivers will have good spring fishing. But two or three years later, the fishing may be the pits because there was not enough water to ensure the survival of trout, salmon, and steelhead fry, or to flush salmon and steelhead smolts out to sea.

This year it looked like a late thaw, and while that might be good for the long term, this trip could be a waste of time. As I drove, the weather kept switching moods like a teenager. Portland was drizzly, Sandy dry. By Mt. Hood it was pouring and the wipers slapped at maximum speed. Less than 20 miles farther, the sky was breaking up into patches of blue mixed with white clouds.

Creekside alders wore a blush of green buds but few leaves. Snow lingered in round patches under tall firs, and Black Butte was draped in white. Farther south, the Sisters poked their three heads into dark clouds. Snow covered their flanks to timberline, and probably below. It boded cold nights, and I doubted the road to Hosmer would be open yet. So much for trophy brook trout.

In the mountains, spring was more promise than reality, but at home tulips and rhododendrons bloomed in the garden, and the maples were leafing out. The lawn was growing, too, and the mower was in its usually spring funk. I knew I should be home fixing it instead of going fishing.

Because I work out of my home, I can often shift my hours around so I can go fishing more often than if I had an 8-5 job. I often chain myself to my desk for a week or two and get a little ahead on my work, then reward myself with an expedition like this one. I'd been a good worker the last couple of weeks, and felt I'd stored up enough karmic balance, or whatever it takes to justify a fishing trip. At least, that's what I told myself. The reasoning went like this: if I stayed home and fixed the lawnmower like a good boy, my psyche would realize that there was no payoff in working hard and getting ahead; therefore I would start to slack off on my work, income would go down, and I could no longer support my family. So this fishing trip wasn't really about big trout. It was integral to the Protestant work ethic, an essential contribution to a strong economy, and a selfless kindness to my wife and two children.

If you're going after big fish, you have to have a mind capable of this kind of reasoning.

Wickiup Reservoir

A roostertail of dust trailed the car as I drove the dirt road that tops Wickiup Dam. The lake was full (a good sign) but appeared rough (not good). I stopped at the south end of the dam for a closer look. A 20 mph gust rocked the car as I got out. White caps rolled onto the dam's rock face.

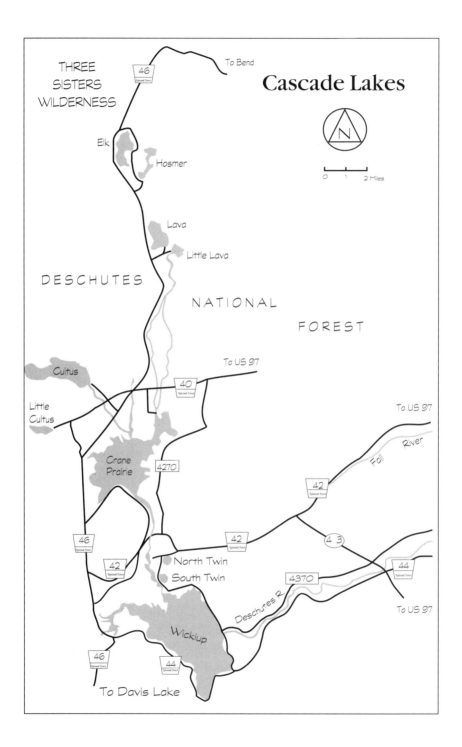

Cascade Lakes

THREE SISTERS WILDERNESS

To Bend

Elk

Hosmer

Lava

Little Lava

DESCHUTES

NATIONAL

FOREST

To US 97

Cultus

Little Cultus

Crane Prairie

To US 97

Fall River

North Twin

South Twin

Deschutes R.

Wickiup

To US 97

To Davis Lake

0   1   2 Miles

46 National Forest
40 National Forest
4270
42 National Forest
42 National Forest
43
46 National Forest
42 National Forest
44 National Forest
4370
46 National Forest
44 National Forest

Windy conditions can be good for trophy brown trout fishing because the cloud cover and waves conceal the wary browns and make them more aggressive. Also, baitfish are dazed and vulnerable in the choppy water, and the browns pick them off like low-hanging fruit. But you can have too much of a good thing, and float tubing under these conditions would have been dumb with a capital "D" and two "M's."

Wickiup often calms by evening, so I fiddled around pitching my tent at the Quinn River campground and fixing an early dinner. When I returned to Wickiup at five o'clock, it was as rough as ever. I contemplated my options: willing browns could probably be found at the sheltered north end of the lake, but they would be 14-16 inch fish—respectable but not the memorable 5-15 pounders I was after; South Twin Lake was close and protected from the wind, but it was a put-and-take fishery, not trophy water; Crane Prairie was a few miles to the north and held large rainbow trout. I asked myself if this trip was a search for big trout or not, then headed to Crane Prairie with hopes of finding an eight-pound rainbow sipping size 18 midges.

What I found was a bunch of frozen anglers. The lake was as cold as a brass toilet seat, as I soon found when water seeped through the seat seam of my aging waders. I gritted my teeth and clenched my butt against cold winds and chilly water.

From the other fishermen I learned that the road to Hosmer Lake was still snow-blocked, confirming my suspicions. I don't know if any of these anglers had leaky waders, but none of them looked happy. The cold had sucked hope out of each one, and few fish came to warm an angler's blood. I saw one small trout caught and spied only three half-hearted rises. Even the fish didn't want to be out in this weather. Singly and in pairs, anglers abandoned Crane Prairie. Each one gave a deep sigh as he climbed stiffly out of his tube and hunched off to a warmer clime.

From the gray sky and chill wind, it was clear this would not be an easy trip. The water was cold and likely to stay that way until June, maybe later. When I left at dark, I vowed not to return to Crane Prairie until the weather and the fish warmed up.

Of my three goals, only the primary one remained: brown trout.

Brown trout were pursued in their native Europe for millennia. By the time they were imported to America in the late 19th century, all the dumb fish had been culled from the gene pool. Initially, American anglers hated the species because they were too hard to catch. The browns were extremely picky about flies, and so wary that one bad cast or one misstep while wading, and they were gone.

A few anglers, however, rose to the challenge and refined their tactics and flies. They showed the way for others, and brown trout became a prized fish. Brown trout forced Americans to be better anglers, and catching a big brown marked you as a fly angler to be reckoned with.

Unlike rainbows, which die at age five or six, brown trout are long-lived. They eat anything and grow huge on a diet of smaller fish. The Oregon state record is a 27-pound monster from Paulina Lake. It was caught on an 11-inch plug, which gives you some idea what size prey big browns are after.

Brown trout are not widely distributed in Oregon's waters. Wickiup, Paulina, East, and Suttle lakes have them, as do the upper Deschutes, Owyhee, and Wood rivers. I've fished all these waters, and in each of them I have seen—and sometimes hooked—brown trout that gave me goosebumps. The browns in Paulina and East lakes are all hatchery-bred, but Wickiup's fish have access to two spawning streams, and Owyhee and Wood river browns are also wild.

If you want to fish for brown trout, you have to push yourself. They are nocturnal, and legal trout fishing in Oregon starts an hour before sunrise and ends an hour after sunset. So if you are serious, you should be on the water ready to fish well before dawn and be prepared to keep casting until you can't see the end of your rod.

I couldn't do it. It was six o'clock when I launched my tube the next morning. That was late, I knew. I should have risen at 3:45 and been fishing by 5:00. But after the cold evening on Crane Prairie, it was too hard to drag my body out of a warm sleeping bag into a freezing, dark morning. Especially when I knew my waders leaked.

I was lucky, my late start not withstanding. Wickiup's strong west wind hadn't started up, and the water was flat and glassy. I cruised the face of the dam, propelling my tube with slow kicks and giving my fly an occasional twitch. In spring the lake is full, and excess water pours from the dam into the upper Deschutes River. This creates a current at the dam face that pulls in baitfish, such as small kokanee and whitefish, and the browns follow the baitfish. Also the water at the dam is deep and rocky, so the big predators have lots of hiding places and ambush sites.

I used my 6-weight fly rod (an 8-weight would have been better) with a Type IV Uniform Sink line. I prefer full-sinking lines for lake fishing because they keep the fly deeper than a sink-tip line. A big wool head sculpin was tied to a short, stout leader.

I had the water to myself. The day progressed from yellow dawn to gray morning. Wind sometimes riffled the surface. I saw one big fish slash through the water 100 feet away. I trolled through the area a couple of times but had no grabs.

When you're pursuing big browns, you need the faith and patience of Job. To keep myself alert, I often imagine what is happening 15 feet below me where my fly cruises the water. It would be highly unusual for it not to pass within striking distance of a fish. No doubt I'd dragged it past several Goliath-sized trout already. I imagined them down there looking at my fly, putting their nose right next to it, deciding whether to inhale it or not. So far, none of those fishy decisions had gone my way, but I kept telling myself that it only takes one willing fish to make an event I'd remember fondly for years.

To keep up my spirits I thought about my last spring trip to Wickiup, at exactly this time of year, at this time of day, at this place, fishing this way with this fly. On that day, one other boat—a small aluminum car topper—worked the same water. Two young men in thick coats were in the boat. Each time they passed, we chatted, and our breath hung in the air. They had been in the area for a week, camping with their wives. Not one fish had graced their hooks. This was their last day, and their wives had issued an ultimatum: come back with something to show or we're not doing this again.

I had persuaded them to go to South Twin Lake where the fishing was much easier, and I think they might have gone if my rod hadn't slammed the water. The guys in the boat hovered close as I played the fish, and after five or ten minutes I had it to the float tube. I tailed the brown—a five or six pounder—and hoisted it up. There was a *thunk-thunk* sound in the aluminum boat; I think it was two jaws hitting the bottom.

At the sight of my fish, these two men got as excited as a roomful of puppies. Here was a trout that would convince any woman that fishing was not a waste of time. They trolled away in search of a fish like mine, their enthusiastic voices fading in the distance. I released the brown and shook my head. Poor guys. They should have gone to South Twin. I hope they got to fish again.

But today it was just me and my leaking waders, slowly kicking back and forth as cold water distributed itself over my lower extremities. By 10:30, hope had faded and my fanny was frozen. I returned to camp for lunch, warmth, and a nap.

Wickiup was calm when I returned in early evening with recharged hope and a re-heated body. I arrived in a rainstorm, but it dissipated by the time I stepped into my tube. A group of young boys were bank fishing in my launch area. Rods rested in forked sticks, and every couple of minutes one of them would wander over and check the rods. The rest of the time they huddled around a fire telling the jokes and stories common to 13-year old boys everywhere. They laughed frequently, with the exaggerated mirth of early adolescence. Every male child goes through this stage, regardless of culture or era. I'm sure all the great men of history—Moses, Alexander the Great, Einstein, and the rest—laughed like this when they were 13.

I talked to the boys about fishing. They'd had no action, so I told a few brown trout stories to keep up their interest (as well as my own). After that, they paid more attention to their rods and sneaked glances at me to see if I had hooked anything.

I kicked along the dam face as I had in the morning, with equal non-results. Once, there was a pull on my line. I pulled back; the line went taut and the rod bowed. On shore, the boys fell silent and turned my way. But it was only a snag.

Evening stretched into dusk. A car had driven up and gathered the boys. I admit to being disappointed. If I was going to hook a nice trout, it would have been more satisfying to have an audience, especially a young impressionable one.

Bob Jones and I had fished here a few years before and were watched by puzzled onlookers. Bob had incubated an idea all winter. "Let's go to Wickiup in early May," he'd told me at work one day. "I think those big browns will be along the face of the dam and can be caught on flies." So we left work early one Friday and headed for Wickiup. That evening, Bob and I were trolling flies from our float tubes. A man and a woman bank-fished from the rocks and watched us with curiosity; at Wickiup, fly fishers are as rare as palm trees.

Just before dusk, Bob said, "I think I'm onto something." I saw the deepest bent rod I'd ever witnessed. I kicked over to Bob's tube, and he handed me his camera. He landed the brown, a big male probably around 8 or 10 pounds, and I snapped the photo. He released the fish. There was a murmur of conversation from the couple fishing on the bank.

Half an hour later, Bob hooked an even bigger fish. I took that photo, too, and when Bob released this trout, the woman on the bank said in amazement, "Do you guys belong to some sort of sportsmen's group or something?"

I thought about Bob's fish as I trolled back and forth along Wickiup's dam. I thought about how the conditions had been similar, except now it was colder, and tried to keep alert for a sudden tightening of the line. I felt a few ticks that might have been short strikes but were probably snags. Rain came and went. A moderate wind blew, and the water looked like hammered metal. The setting sun turned the clouds pink, then brighter pink, then yellow. Darkness followed. My hands were raw and chapped, and I felt like I had spent four hours sitting on an ice cube. Sometime after 9:00 I gave it up.

When you pursue trophy fish—memorable fish—you trade quantity for quality. Your intellect can easily grasp this concept. But when you've spent twelve hours sitting in cold water with leaky waders and haven't had a single strike, it's hard to convince your frozen butt that you *have* an intellect.

That night I lay in my down sleeping bag wondering what to do next. The cold and the wind had sapped my enthusiasm for Wickiup's browns and Crane's rainbows, but an alternative came to mind: Suttle Lake. I'd never fished it but had always wanted to. I began constructing justifications in my mind. *Suttle is small, so the waves won't be bad,* I told myself. *It's rumored to have some big brown trout. What's more, it's at the summit of Santiam Pass—on the way home.* This latter reason loomed larger as I dwelt on it. Warmth, company, good food, soft bed. Dry shorts. Suttle Lake would put me closer to all these. Shortly after dawn I broke camp and headed there.

Suttle Lake

It didn't take long to see that the Suttle Lake lodge had had a checkered past, looked forward to a great future, but had an abysmal present. I wandered through a confusion of old lumber, sawdust, power tools, and sawhorses to find the owner. He stopped his remodeling project and greeted me with bon homie and answered my questions about the lake's fishing.

"There's some big ones out there," he said as he filled out my free membership card in the Friends of Suttle Lake Society. "They hang out in the east end of the lake."

My jaw tightened. The west wind still blew hard and was piling white caps onto the eastern shore, so this looked like a repeat of Wickiup and Crane Prairie. I headed out anyway and launched the Klamath.

For a change of pace, I laid down the fly rod and trolled a spoon from my ultralight spinning rod. Trolling gave me the opportunity to scrunch down inside layers of clothing. The only parts of me that moved were my left hand as it steered the boat and my eyes as I scanned the water for fish.

I thought I saw a head-and-tail rise in the waves, but couldn't be sure. Browns will often come out in rough conditions and feed in the waves, so I told myself it could have been a fish. The rod added its vote five minutes later when it gave a quick jerk-and-release that seemed too animated to be a snag. Not long after, I had a solid hookup and brought a 16-inch brown trout to the boat.

This was a decent-sized fish for the ultralight. Using it for much bigger prey would have been like pursuing a rhinoceros with a .22. By late afternoon I'd had a few more grabs and landed four fish, all between 12 and 16 inches.

Then I saw it, in the crest of a wave, slicing through the water with no effort, mouth open as if in pursuit of baitfish. It was a truly big brown trout—easily 25 inches, maybe 30. White belly, yellow-brown sides, dark back, red spots—there was no mistaking it. Or was there? I stared into the water where I thought I'd seen the fish, but all I saw were green waves flecked with white, the interplay of light and shadow in moving water. Was it really a big brown? Or was it more wish than fish, more illusive than elusive?

By late afternoon, the clouds were breaking up and the wind quieting. I told myself it could be a calm evening with just enough wind riffle to make the fishing both pleasant and productive. As I glanced at the clouds, I recalled my all-time most memorable brown trout. It was an August day the previous summer, and my fly rod and I were at East Lake. A few clouds had piled up over Paulina Peak and drifted over the lake. I parked the Klamath on a sandy beach at midday and took a shoreside nap.

When I awoke, I saw a huge cloud formation. To me, a cloud is a cloud; I'm not a person who finds shapes in them. But this chunk of sculpted cumulus was a perfect fish, a gigantic fish, a trophy brown trout with a clearly defined tail, dorsal fin, arched back, and head. It even had scales.

I lay on my back and looked at it with religious awe. Clearly, God was sending me a sign that I was going to hook a big brown trout that very evening. Believing in a gracious God, I figured He'd tell me what the fish was taking, so I looked past the perfectly formed head to the mouth. There, between the jaws was another small cloud. *Leech?* I wondered. *Matuka? Woolhead sculpin? Muddler Minnow? Woolly Bugger perhaps?* I squinted at the little cloud, trying to discern which of my many flies it most resembled.

It was shaped exactly like a U-20 Flatfish, a lure I didn't possess.

No such omens came from the clouds over Suttle Lake, and I was on my own to figure out which lure or fly to use. By the time I drove back to my campsite to fix dinner, I'd decided to fish through the evening using my fly rod. I would return at sunrise and fish for a few hours before heading home. Catching some fish and the sight (maybe) of a truly big trout had refreshed my waning enthusiasm.

Even rocks erode in the wind, however, and my enthusiasm for memorable trout proved less durable than granite. The westerly gale returned, and when I put away the last of the cook pots, I also took down the tent. I'd fish the evening, then go home.

When I reached the boat ramp, I found that the latch on the outboard motor was bent, and I couldn't lower it. It was an easy problem to fix—*if* I'd had the right tools, which I didn't.

The fitful wind had been quiet for a few minutes, so I decided to use the float tube. I struggled into my waders, flinching as their cold, wet interior contacted my warm, dry exterior. I was reaching for my boots when a wind gust rocked the car.

That blast snipped the last frayed thread of my ambition. I'd had it with cold and wind. I wanted a hot shower, good food, and a dry butt. I packed everything back into the car and headed home.

Somewhere on I-5 south of Salem, against a background glare of oncoming headlights, I had recurring flashbacks of a big brown trout sliding through the crest of wave in Suttle Lake. The next day it was there whenever I closed my eyes. Months later I could recall it perfectly but could never say for sure that it was more than a trick of light and shadow played on a mind eager to be deceived.

On this trip, my most memorable fish may never have existed.

4

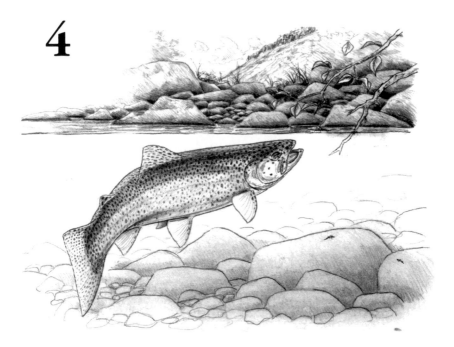

The Road To Mecca

Late May, Deschutes River near Mecca Flat

The road to Mecca is dirt and has many potholes. It's not hard to find, but you have to take its existence on faith because there are no signs. It's off the main highway, US 26, just east of the "Rainbow Market." A humble but well-traveled road, it begins easily enough, then gains elevation and turns very rough and narrow. Mecca is a peaceful place, uplifting in a mystical way. While it's not heaven, it's only half a mile from it.

I usually make a pilgrimage to Mecca in late spring, when the desert air is filled with the strong scent of sage and the songs of meadowlarks. The grass is green and tall then, and there's something about the slant of the sun at the end of May, the way the light hits the canyon walls or picks out the brief green fuzz of the hills. The spring light at Mecca is soft and vibrant. If I had to assign a human quality to it, I'd pick hope, although that probably reflects my feelings about angling for the river's wild trout.

Trout were not on the minds of those who named this place, but hope certainly was. From 1910 to 1912, thousands of men sweated, shoveled, picked, blasted, and hammered for three years until they'd punched a railroad through the rugged Deschutes River canyon. Their goal was to reach a big flat about 100 miles upstream from the river's mouth. Once they reached that flat they'd be out of the canyon, and the most grueling work would be done. The place became such a desirable goal that it took on religious symbolism, and they named it Mecca Flat.

In recent times, fly anglers have been Mecca's chief visitors. On the lower Deschutes, this is the farthest upstream that most bank anglers fish. It's possible to drop your fly above here, but the opportunities are limited and the traffic noise annoying at best.

Mecca Flat is broad and long, but within a mile the canyon walls pull in like the sides of an hour glass. There are good trails on the east bank, and you can walk downstream seven miles— all the way to Trout Creek—and drop your fly into gentle-flowing runs, alder-shaded bank water, and backeddies.

On the Deschutes, late May means the salmonfly hatch, an event anticipated by many fly anglers. Salmonflies are the adult stage of the giant stonefly. Nymphs of the species live in the river for three years, crawling among fist-sized boulders to gobble smaller insects, and eventually growing to be one of the biggest macro-invertebrates in North America.

Beginning in May, mature nymphs over two inches long crawl out of the river, climb up a stalk of grass or an alder trunk, and the adult emerges. Emergence is a long process, fascinating to watch if you're into bugs like I am. First, the back of the nymph's exoskeleton splits and the adult's thorax pokes out. It is

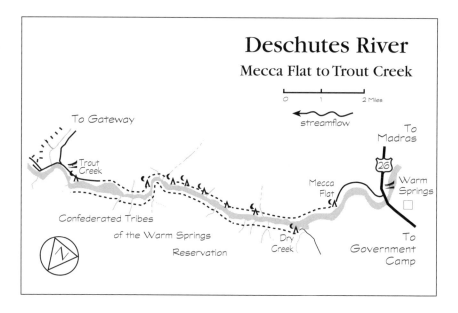

Deschutes River

Mecca Flat to Trout Creek

0   1   2 Miles

To Gateway

streamflow

To Madras

Trout Creek

26

Mecca Flat

Warm Springs

Confederated Tribes
of the Warm Springs
Reservation

Dry Creek

To Government Camp

soon followed by the head. Then in a process that can take twenty minutes or more, the salmonfly pulls a few legs out and laboriously extracts its long antennae from the shuck. The wings begin to unfurl, and the abdomen pulls free. The fully emerged adult lingers on grass stems overnight while blood pressure pumps up its wings, and by morning it is ready to fly. Emergence is long and exhausting, and the salmonflies are helpless throughout. That's why it happens at night, when birds and other predators can't pick them off.

The adults are orange-bodied, double-winged, and as big as the nymphs from which they hatched. They're poor flyers and spend most of their time crawling on shoreside vegetation looking for a mate. When the hatch is on, bankside trees and grass are thick with them. With each gust of wind, a few are shaken off and fall onto the river. In the afternoon and evening, females carrying fertilized eggs settle on the water and drop the future of their species into the river.

As you'd imagine, a bug this size is a tempting tidbit for a trout, and big rainbows move close to the bank and gorge on them. Anglers are next up the food chain, for who can resist casting a two-inch long dry fly to aggressive trout?

At one time, the salmonfly season was a big deal to the Deschutes' ace anglers, something they looked forward to all year. It became such a big deal that it turned into a zoo. If there is a time of year that the casual fly angler comes to the Deschutes, this is it—and there are a lot more casual anglers than experts. Most of the river's best anglers now stay home during the salmonfly hatch, partly because of the crowds and partly because of who's in the crowd.

There's less snobbery in that than it sounds. Many of those who show up for the hatch do not yet know how to take care of the river, and they become ignorant abusers of its fragile ecology. The experts have a religious zeal about protecting their beloved river, and during the salmonfly hatch they feel like priests whose temple has been overrun by barbarian hoards.

Most beginners and casual anglers would be better if they knew what to do. But there are others who don't *want* to know better, and the bozo index (number of discarded beer cans, multiplied by instances of boorish behavior, and divided by river miles) reaches its peak on the Memorial Day weekend.

For years, my preferred way to take advantage of the salmonflies was to cast nymphs beginning in April. I'd tie on a big Girdlebug or Kaufmann's Stone and let it drift near the bottom along current seams and through rocky runs. If I got in on the dry fly action in late May, fine; if not, I didn't miss it because I'd had my fun earlier.

A few years ago I even gave up on spring nymphing for rainbows. I had talked to enough fish biologists that I came to understand how hard spawning can be on a trout's body. I concluded that they didn't need the added stress of a tug-of-war at the end of my line. Also, trout are concentrated over their spawning beds in the spring, and wading through them risks damaging the fish of the future.

Now I go to lakes and other rivers in the early spring, focusing on brown trout and brook trout because they're fall spawners. When I turn to river-dwelling rainbows in late spring, my strategy is to cast a dry or near-surface fly into backeddies. This does two things: first, it keeps me off the spawning beds; second, the dark spawners prefer to hunker on the bottom and seldom rise to a dry fly, so I only catch fresh fish.

The flaw in this strategy is that from mid-April to mid-May, the river and its backeddies are full of salmon and steelhead smolts heading for the ocean. These little guys throw themselves onto your hook with gay abandon, often with disastrous consequences for themselves.

I've come to the point where I avoid the Deschutes altogether in early spring because there is almost no way to fish without messing up my future sport.

My vehicle for getting to Mecca was a Toyota Land Cruiser, a car that had been my fishing transportation for eight years. I've never owned a more reliable car, nor one better suited to my way of fishing. This model year was the first for a new engine and transmission. A couple of years later, Toyota upgraded the Land Cruiser and turned it into a luxury car that was too fancy and expensive for me. Fishing cars are important, and I had taken good care of this one because I intended to use it another ten years.

It was nearly 7:00 in the evening when I turned onto the road to Mecca. I was playing the ascetic and had left behind as many material possessions as I dared. No boat, no tent, little food, only one camera and one fly rod. I'd even left my raingear behind, a decision that seemed less than inspired since the only cloud in Oregon was parked over Mecca and was dripping big drops of rain. Fortunately, the cloud soon dumped its load and evaporated. By the time I'd donned my waders and eaten a peanut butter sandwich, the sky was clear.

On my way to the river, I noticed an array of objects scattered atop one camper's picnic table: a spinning rod, an electric blender, various alcoholic beverages, and a set of golf clubs. I don't know what this angler expected to find here; Mecca has neither electric outlets nor putting greens.

I found the river a bit high, but not bad for this time of year. The water temperature was 50 degrees, which is two degrees less than optimum for salmonfly activity. Mecca Flat is close to the dam, so the water is colder than anywhere else on the river. I speculated that several miles downstream the salmonflies might be more active. Still, there were a few in Mecca's alders, and that gave me hope, however faint.

There is some good fishing right at the Mecca campground, but I pointed my feet toward the backeddies. These begin half a mile from Mecca, and as far as I'm concerned, they are heaven. Some people don't like to fish backeddies, and it's true that the contrary currents can be devilish tricky to cast to. The waters eddy and spin and come back on themselves like a pack of Talmudic scholars. Getting a good drift calls for careful reading of the current, slack line casts, and a willingness to recognize that the best fish may be impossible to reach. Nevertheless, these circling waters are some of my favorite places on the river.

As I walked to the first backeddy, the sun slipped near the western rimrock, leaving the west bank and half the river in shade but lighting the eastern cliffs with a warm yellow light. The grass was thick and green, with yellow heads beginning to appear. Crickets began their dusk chorus.

When I reached my goal, I found a drift boat parked there and a tent set up. I asked the campers if they were planning to fish. They said they were done for the day, so the water was mine.

I approach these backeddies with care, especially this first one. I crouch low the last 50 feet and get down on my knees when I fish. Some people think I'm praying for trout (like that's the only way I'll catch one), but my posture is more for stealth than penitence. Mecca's trout see a lot of anglers and are easily spooked, so a low profile keeps me out of their view. Even so, I saw a nice one slip away at my arrival.

I planned to start with a dry salmonfly and see how receptive the trout were to the pattern, but when I opened the fly box I saw only two bedraggled Madam Xs; I'd left an entire fly box at home, the one with most of my salmonfly patterns. While I contemplated this strategic blunder, I looked over the river and saw a few adult salmonflies drop to the water and flutter on the surface. They drifted for 20 yards, making a huge fuss all the way, but were unmolested by trout. Apparently the fish were not yet focused on the big bugs.

A few trout rose in the backeddy, but no insects were visible on the surface. Both caddis and midges were in the air, so I had two choices: a size 18 midge or a size 14 caddis. I opted for the fly that was easier to tie on in fading light and threaded a brown Soft Hackle onto my leader. Soft Hackles are good producers on the Deschutes. The river is caddis-rich, and the fly imitates both the pupal form of the insect and the adult females that swim underwater to lay their eggs.

I cast into the current seam on the outside edge of the backeddy. It swept across the seam, then dangled along its inside edge. I cast several times, lengthening the line by three feet with each throw.

This is a really stupid way to fish. It requires little finesse or skill, but it works, as a 12-inch rainbow demonstrated on my fourth or fifth cast. Half a dozen more trout picked up my fly as I kept working down the seam. They were all 12 inches or less, fish that were not yet old enough to spawn. Only one smolt was among them.

A large splash in the river caught my attention. I looked just past the campers' driftboat to see a salmonfly drifting down, then disappear in a swirl. I changed to a heavier leader and tied on one of the ragged Madam Xs. As I prepared to make my first cast to the bigger fish, one of the campers came down to fetch an item from his driftboat. By the time he was done banging around, the trout was thoroughly spooked.

I changed leaders again and put the Soft Hackle back on, but before I could cast it there was another sploosh in the river.

The big trout (or at least, *a* big trout) was feeding again. Once more, I changed leaders and tied on the salmonfly pattern. Once more, a camper came down to the driftboat and spooked the fish just as I was ready to cast. I couldn't get mad; it was their campwater, and I was a guest on it. It was just one of those things that happens when the river is crowded.

By now it was too dark to change leaders and flies, so I gave it up. Crickets and grasshoppers were making a racket in the grass, and a few stars winked in the east. I saw one of the kids from camp silhouetted against the indigo sky, all akimbo as he played hacky-sack.

Shortly after I went to bed in the Land Cruiser, a front blew in. It whistled past the window cracks and rocked the car. Several times I was awakened by rain pelting on the roof, but it never lasted long, and by morning the air was clear and heating up.

After a monastically simple breakfast of oatmeal and a banana, I hot-footed back to the backeddies. Hot-footed is an accurate verb in this case: it was a warm day, and several times I waded into the river to prevent meltdown. The cold, damp May seemed to be yielding to better weather.

I worked my way downstream, one eddy at a time, until I was a couple of miles from Mecca Flat. Not much was happening. I picked up one trout each on a Beadhead Nymph, a Madam X, and an Elk Hair Caddis. None of the fish were big, though, and I longed for a prime 15- or 16-inch redside. I knew where their spawning beds were, and there are some techniques for taking them when they're on the redds (none of which I will mention here nor anywhere else, and none of which I use myself anymore).

I met one angler who boasted of picking up several big fish on a spinner. I stood on a high bank and had a clear view of where he was fishing: it was over a major spawning bed. He either had no idea—or cared little—about the damage he might be doing.

When I returned to camp, the salmonflies were out in force.

Warming water had given many the urge to leave the river for their brief life on the wing, and the alders were thick with big, newly hatched insects.

Salmonflies are the friendliest non-biting bug on earth. They land on you and walk around on your arms and face like you were just another kind of tree. If you're bothered by having a dozen or so two-and-a-half inch long insects continually creeping over your body, don't come to the Deschutes in late May.

I ate my lunch in the shade of an alder as salmonflies crawled up my arms and across the back of my neck. Some landed on my hat, and every now and then I looked up to see a pair of waving, two-inch long antennae and a buggy head peering at me over the brim. Once, I heard a thumping sound on top of my head. I took off the hat and found two salmonflies vigorously mating there. I'm an amateur entomologist, but I draw the line at being a No-Tell Motel for them. I gently moved the lovers to an alder branch. They hardly missed a beat.

I figured this trip was just a few days too early. Half a week more and gravid females would be fluttering over the water, driving the trout into fits of gluttonous glory. They were probably already doing that a few more miles downstream where the water had been just enough warmer for a few more days.

I finished the day with a return to the backeddies, kneeling at the edge of each one. I once heard a story about a Muslim who made a pilgrimage to Mecca—the one in Saudi Arabia—and shuffled the entire distance on his knees as a sign of humility and homage. Because I approach the backeddies of Mecca—the one on the Deschutes—with the same posture, it's easy to tell which waders are mine: the ones with the heavily patched knees.

On my way back to the car at dusk, I heard a huge splash in the river, then another. A few salmonflies were settling on the water, and big trout were coming up to them. My two Madam Xs had been sacrificed on tree branches earlier in the day, and there was little I could do without the right flies. Besides, I'd had a good time and felt satisfied. Soon it would be time for the pale morning duns of June and the caddis of July. The crowds would

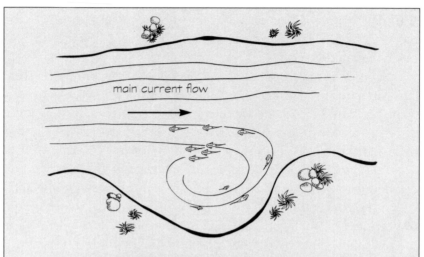

Fly Fishing the Backeddies

Backeddies are excellent concentrators of drifting insects and other trout food. The drawing shows the most common places to find trout in a backeddy.

The trick to fly fishing a backeddy is to get a drag-free drift. This can be extremely difficult because the prime lies usually have contrary currents. Sometimes it is best to cast only to places where you can get a good drift and forget the rest, regardless of how many big trout are rising out there.

One good approach to backeddies is to watch the foam lines, which often shift around. Trout will be feeding in the foam line, so put your fly there. Sometimes you'll see a big "push" of foam. Upwelling currents have concentrated the foam (and insects), and trout feed at the leading edge of the push. Wait patiently until the push forms, then cast to the front of it as it comes toward you. Usually, the current will float your fly with little drag.

Each backeddy is different. Pick a few good ones, then learn exactly where to stand (or kneel) so you are hidden from the trout and can get a drag-free drift. In most backeddies, there will be only two or three good spots. Above all, recognize that there are some excellent trout lies in which you will never get a good drift. Pass these by and move on to more productive places.

diminish, and the fish were getting brighter and stronger. I'd be back.

A week later I spoke to friend who had drifted the river the same days I was there. "About four miles below Mecca," he said, "the salmonflies were thick as lawyers. Trout everywhere. I never had so many big fish on a dry fly."

If I'd drifted the river I'd have been into big fish, too. Or if I'd driven to Trout Creek and walked upstream. But I've never been fond of the Trout Creek water. The backeddies are not as good, the light is not the same in spring. And if I'd drifted I'd have missed things you only see when you walk.

I didn't regret my spring hajj to Mecca any more than I regretted leaving the spawners alone. I'm sure that to some it seems like self-flagellation or hair-shirt Puritanism. But every pilgrim has his own vision of heaven—and knows what road will take him there.

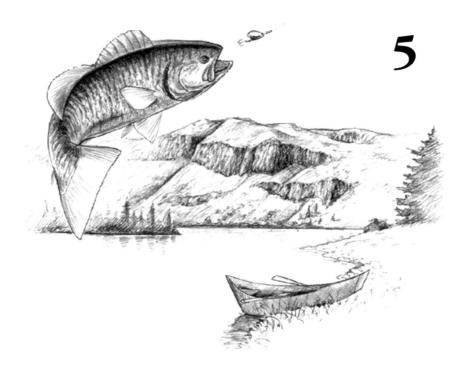

5

River of the Naked Runner

Early June, John Day

Try next to that patch of foam," Dave said. Great minds, and all that . . . my small silver spinner was already heading in that direction. A couple of cranks, then a sudden pull bent my ultralight spinning rod into a semi-circle. A two-pound smallmouth leapt from the water with my spinner dangling from his mouth. "Got him!" I said.

"Really?" Dave said, pulling on the oars as he guided the boat downstream. "You've got a fish?"

"Yeah." The bass came downriver with us and was soon near the boat.

"You really have a fish on?" Dave said again.

"Yes. Yes. Why don't you believe me?"

"I'll be damned."

"Why are you so surprised?" I said as I grabbed the smallmouth by the lip and hoisted him up. "Put the oars down and take a photo."

"You actually caught one?"

My companion was Dave Hughes, probably the most prolific writer of fly-fishing books in the history of the sport. Although our senses of humor warp in different directions, there are common elements, and his disbelief in the existence of my bass revealed a skepticism based on several years of reciprocal spoofing.

We were in Dave's 12-foot Santiam Drifter, taking a three-day, 48-mile float down the John Day River. This part of Northeast Oregon is rugged country. Although none of these mountains are as tall or massive as the newer peaks of the Cascades, they are steep and rocky. A check of the map revealed that one of them has the whimsical name of *Hoogie Doogie Mountain*, a clear one-up over its more spectacular cousins to the east, most of which were named for presidents and naval bureaucrats.

This is arid country, but the little rain that falls eventually finds its way into the several forks of the John Day. By the time they've all merged into the mainstem, a major river has been created. One distinction of the John Day is that it carries more sediment for its size than any other river in Oregon.

Wild steelhead and salmon migrate to and from the John Day, but the resident gamefish are smallmouth bass. The bass are not native to the river (or anywhere else in the Northwest), but they thrive in it. Unlike the Deschutes, the John Day has few springs to cool its waters. In addition, irrigators draw extensively from the river. The result is that summer flows are low and warm—conditions ill-suited to trout, but tolerable for bass.

The John Day country is beautiful, reminiscent of the lower Deschutes, yet different. The river has been eroding the lava that surrounds it for about three times as long as the Deschutes has been sculpting its own basalt-ribbed course. The result is a broader

John Day River

Service Creek to Clarno

canyon with more rounded hills. It feels less rugged here than on the lower Deschutes. If you love the Deschutes, you should visit the John Day for a vision of the future; another ten million years, give or take a few dozen millennia, and the Deschutes canyon will look like this.

It was early June when Dave and I launched his boat near the tiny community of Service Creek. Spring grass, sage, and juniper made a symphony of greens. The texture of the steep hills was easy to discern: wherever topography funneled water, juniper gathered to

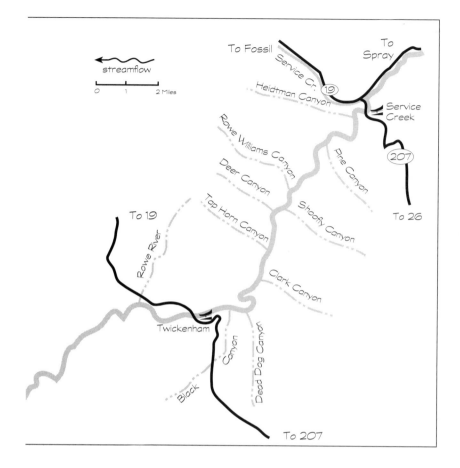

make evergreen rivers. Red-tinged cheat grass harmonized with the greens, and here and there a red cinder cone added a reminder of the region's violent past.

Not all the violence was in the past, however. Just before we arrived, a thunderstorm rolled through and left the river high and muddy—and the fishing bad. A few days earlier the river was probably perfect, and a few days later it would be so again. But now . . . Three weeks earlier, while on the Deschutes, I'd hoped the long, wet spring was over. Apparently not.

Dave and I took turns rowing while the other cast to bassy-looking water. Mostly we fished from the boat, plopping our lures into likely places as we drifted by, but sometimes we'd stop and fish from the bank. At one stop, I tossed my spinner into a patch of promising water and watched a bass shoot from under a rock ledge and nail the lure right at my feet. I love it when they do that. Dave picked up a few fish on plastic Mr. Twisters, but bright spinners seemed to work best. We each carried a fly rod and some bass poppers, but felt lures would work best because the water was so high and turbid.

By noon I'd discovered several things: first, most bass were along the edges where quiet water lay near faster current; second, patches of foam were the best clue to where this kind of water could be found; third, a small silver spinner worked best in the off-color water; fourth, there were a lot of snags on which I was losing spinners; fifth, I'd exhausted my supply of spinners by noon of the first day of a three-day trip. This was the third time this year that I had run out of the right fly or lure. I wrote a note on my clipboard: "Make spinners. Tie flies. Stop going off half-cocked."

Except for the March brown hatch, all my fishing this year had been solitary. This trip made up for it in spades. Not only was I with Dave, but we had an entourage of five others. There were Scott Stouder, an outdoor writer from Corvallis; Pat Wray and Ken Durbin, both of the Oregon Department of Fish and Wildlife; Stump, a friend of Pat's whose real name I don't think I ever heard; and Jim Fife. The seven of us were distributed among two canoes, a full-sized drift boat, and Dave's mini-drifter.

This section of the John Day has few tough rapids, with only a couple of class IIs and what might pass for a III. The river is considered runnable when the flow is between 1,500 cfs (cubic feet per second) and 6,000 cfs. After the rainstorm, it was around 4,500 cfs. That's high for canoe passage, as we soon found out.

Dave and I had passed through the first class II, then pulled over to watch as the two canoes negotiated the standing waves and rocks. Ken was first. He was alone, and we had some of his gear. Even so, the rapids half-filled his canoe. Then came Pat and Jim. With the extra weight of another man, they rode lower in the water—and got lower as they progressed through the rapids. First, we saw a canoe and two guys paddling. Then it was half a canoe and two guys paddling. Then just two guys up to their chests in the river. But still paddling.

Others before us had not been so fortunate. At one stop, I found a third of a canoe rocking gently in shallow water. Apparently someone had tried to run the river when it was too high and had hit a rock. Enough slime had grown on the canoe to show that this had happened a few weeks before, and we didn't need to search the river for stranded paddlers in dripping clothes. It was a warning, though: know the river and know your limits.

The first non-Indians who came here didn't have dripping clothes, however. They had no clothes at all.

John Day and Ramsey Cook were two trappers from Astor's outpost at the mouth of the Columbia. In 1811 they were separated from two other members of their exploration party and almost died of starvation. Friendly Indians rescued them and sent them on their way, but they soon ran into a party of less-kindly locals, a group that had been badly treated by whites. Day and Cook were captured, and all their possessions—including clothing—were taken from them.

The two men spent four days running naked through the wilderness to avoid the hostile Indians. Eventually they came across the friendly Indians who had helped them before. They were fed and clothed, and later met an overland expedition coming down the Columbia River. Day and Cook were described as emaciated and wretched beyond the point of recognition. They were rescued where a major river entered the Columbia, a river that became known as John Day's River.

What I don't understand is why the cartographers kept both the surname and Christian name of the unfortunate trapper. Perhaps it was some Victorian sensibility, like they could hide his nakedness by covering the river with his names. I can think of no other Oregon explorer who was honored in this way.

We picked a broad flat for our first campsite, and Dave and I pitched our tent near a juniper tree. Although we fish together several times a year, this was the first time Dave and I had actually camped with each other. Both of us do this sort of thing a lot, and it's always interesting to compare notes, especially about cooking.

"What's that," I asked Dave. He was dipping bass filets in some white, crinkly substance before frying them.

"Panko. It's Japanese. Makes good, crisp fillets."

"Looks good. Say, I like that wood kitchen box. Make it yourself?"

"Yeah. It's handy. I can fit all my plates, cups, pots, utensils, and condiments in there. The Coleman fits on top. I like those water bottles you use."

"I went to those when I floated the Deschutes a lot three summers ago. Five gallons of water weighs over forty pounds. There's no sense carrying that much water up the bank every night, then most of it back down the next day. I found these 3-gallon jugs and use them instead. I gave up on those plastic blobs, though. They spring a leak if you look at them funny."

"I hear you. Have some salad."

"How'd you do that dressing?"

We continued discussing campcraft in a long *Martha Stewart Goes Bassin'* sort of dialogue.

About every half hour on this trip, Dave would mention something that reminded him of a fishing trip he'd taken with Masako Tani, a Japanese woman he'd had a serious relationship with. It had been over four years since they'd broken up, and I'd never heard him talk so much about her. Later, I examined a book Dave was reading, and the bookmark fell out. It was an airline boarding pass from a recent flight to Hawaii. Hmm. A romantic island half-way between Japan and Oregon. Hmm again.

After dinner, Dave and I joined the others in a general bull session, one of those so-called male-bonding campfire chats that ranged through bass, deer, trout, salmon, elk, grouse, sheep, wilderness experiences, wildlife management, gun-control, the failings of the NRA, bear attacks, and helicopters. The latter came because Stump and Pat had both been Marine pilots in Vietnam. During the fall of Saigon, when helicopters were picking refugees from the roof of the US embassy, Pat was one of the pilots. But his most terrifying helicopter ride was in Canada when Stump had the stick.

It happened on what was supposed to be a military training exercise on the rugged coast of British Columbia. Pat had spotted a river that looked like it might have good fishing and convinced Stump to land in a clearing and drop off Pat and a couple of other would-be anglers. "It'll be good training," was the excuse.

When Stump came back for them later, the air temperature had soared, and his helicopter couldn't get enough lift to climb out of the clearing. He was able to reach 50 feet, then follow the river toward the ocean. They came around a bend, and smack in the middle of the river was a small island with a 150-foot fir tree. There wasn't enough room to go down either side, not enough air to go over, and even a helicopter can't stop on a dime. Pat had but one thought: "We're dead."

Stump flipped the helicopter on its side and slipped past the tree edgewise, his rotors barely clearing the ground.

Toward sunset, Dave and I took a hike to the top of a nearby hill. Every fall, Dave hunts deer at a ranch a few miles downstream from our campsite. He wanted to climb this knoll and look for deer and antelope. Glassing for deer is Dave's favorite non-fishing activity. He trains his binoculars on each gully and hillside and tries to divine where the big bucks hang out.

I enjoyed the view, but my interest was different than Dave's. I look over country like this and think how I would love to come here with my horse and ride through the juniper-strewn canyons and across the treeless hills.

From the top of the knoll we had a full view of the river canyon, and it was a delight to the eyes. The gray clouds that had hung over us in the morning had moved on, and the few clouds that remained were small and white. The low angle of the sun created shadows that highlighted the textures of the canyon. Eroded spires, reefs of columnar basalt, red cinder cones, towering cliffs, rounded hummocks, and steep side canyons stood in relief. Lupine and paintbrush were just beginning to bloom and took on a yellow tint as the sun dipped to the horizon. We even found a few small cactus.

After Dave spent five minutes scanning the hill, I asked if he saw anything.

"I think I've got an antelope," he said.

I followed the line of his binoculars but couldn't tell anything for sure. "Which way is it moving?"

"It's not," Dave said. He looked a little longer. "I think it's a rock. Maybe it's a petrified antelope." He glassed a different part of the hill. "There's some deer. Four of them."

"Are they petrified, too?"

"They're more real than that big bass you told me you caught. Have a look."

He handed me the binoculars, and I saw them, too.

"They come down at night and feed in the alfalfa fields. Alfalfa farmers are the deer hunter's best friend."

"Speaking of best friends, are you seeing Masako again?"

Dave scanned the hills some more. "Maybe," he said.

On the way down the hill, Dave found an antler from a four-point buck.

"Are you going to keep it?" I asked. He handed it to me. "Thanks," I said. "I think Holly might like it for a decoration in her room." Holly is my youngest daughter, a good kid with a passion for horses.

"How old is she?" Dave asked.

"Sixteen. Just got her driver's license. One day you're carrying them in your arms, the next day they want the keys to the car."

Fishing improved as the river continued to drop. The next morning, bass and a few squawfish grabbed our lures. Squawfish are vora-

Floating the John Day River

The most common put-ins and take-outs on the John Day River are Service Creek (river mile 158), Twickenham (mile 144), Clarno (mile 110), Cottonwood Bridge (mile 40). Most river drifters do a one-day trip (Service Creek to Twickenham), a three-day (Service Creek to Clarno), or a week (Clarno to Cottonwood).

May and early June are the best times to run the river. The flow should be over 1,500 cfs (cubic feet per second) and less than 6,000. Anything over 4,000 cfs is heavy water and requires a skilled oarsman; leave your canoe at home if the river is that high. The best levels for drifting are between 2,000 cfs and 2,500 cfs. You can check the flow by calling the National Weather Service at 503/261-9246.

Between Service Creek and Clarno, there are a few class II or III rapids, the difficulty depending on water volume. Below Clarno, the only difficult water is Clarno rapids, but it can be a class IV passage.

There is a store at Service Creek that can arrange shuttles.

There are few developed campgrounds on the John Day, but river drifters can camp anywhere that is not private land. Excellent campsites are not difficult to find. Be prepared with lots of drinking water, take extreme care with fire and flame, and know the rudiments of personal hygiene when there are no flush toilets or outhouses. If you have any questions on this latter point, get the descriptively named book How to Shit in the Woods, *published by Ten Speed Press and available at most outdoor stores.*

Art Campbell has written a good guide book for the John Day. Published by Frank Amato Publications, it includes maps, guidelines, photos, and history.

cious predators, but are not valued as a gamefish. In the afternoon, another species of fish revealed itself. We'd switched to fly rods and stopped to fish some bank water where we'd seen rises. Close examination revealed the rises were from chub, a small fish even less desirable than squawfish. Under the chub there seemed to be more activity. I rigged my fly rod with a silver Zonker, cast beyond the pod of rising fish, and let the fly sink a few seconds before retrieving it. There was a sudden take, and I soon had a nice bass on the bank.

"I think I know what the bass and squawfish forage on," I said. I opened the mouth of the bass and showed it to Dave. A small, silvery chub lay just past the gills.

"That's probably why those silver spinners worked so well," Dave said. "Of course bass will eat anything that looks remotely alive."

This theory was thoroughly tested the next day. The river had continued to drop and clear, so we stuck with the fly rods, only now we tied on small bass poppers. The action came fast. Nearly every time a cast landed in bassy water there would be an explosion as a smallmouth grabbed the popper.

On this final day we often floated past vertical cliffs of columnar basalt. These created micro-eddies and patches of stillwater, and in each one there was at least one smallmouth. The fly rod was the perfect tool to take advantage of this. Because we didn't need to reel in before casting, it took just a quick flip of the line to put the popper in the right place. Let it sit, then a quick twitch, and blam!—another bass.

One of us would row while the other fished. The oarsman's job was to stay the same distance from the bank so the caster never had to change the length of line and could place the fly within a few inches of the cliff. When we were in the right water, bass were guaranteed.

On the drive home, Dave and I made plans to come back to the John Day. We'd seen enough of the river to want a return trip under better conditions.

"Two weeks ought to do it," Dave said. "It should be a good color, still have enough water, and be a couple of degrees warmer."

"Bass on every cast," I said. "A sure thing."

Two weeks later we camped next to the boat ramp, ready to

launch the next morning. The weather forecast was vague, but when we arrived the sun was setting into a blue horizon. The river was clear and at a good height—perfect shape for fishing. Nothing could keep the bass off our flies and lures.

Nothing but the last storm of spring.

During the night, rain rolled off the tent like we'd pitched it under a fire hose. By morning the river had muddied and risen a foot. As we drifted, squalls of heavy rain alternated with breaks in the clouds. Instead of shorts and T-shirts, we wore long johns and raingear. We picked up a few bass, but we both knew what we'd find the next morning.

The rain sluiced down Hoogie Doogie Mountain and all the other hills. It swelled every creek in the basin, which then dumped their loads into the John Day. When we arose, the river was three feet higher than when we'd gone to bed. Visibility was slightly better than a brick wall.

There was no point in staying. We drifted 32 miles to the Clarno take-out and drove home. Spring had given us one last licking.

Jurassic Fish

June, near Scotts Mills, Willamette Valley

My red Land Cruiser lay on its side in the ditch. Every body panel was dented, bent, twisted, or broken. The roof made a sharp V into the passenger compartment that a few hours earlier had held my daughter Holly and three teen-aged friends.

I walked up the road to where the curving skid marks began, then followed them as they swerved to within three feet of the road edge. Narrow shoulder of soft dirt. No guard rail. Fifty feet straight down to a creek flowing over bedrock. I felt nauseated and incredibly weary.

Through winter and spring, Holly had worked most weekends

as a wrangler at Butte Creek Ranch, a Boy Scout facility south of Portland. On a Saturday night when I was camped on the John Day, she drove three fellow wranglers to dinner in nearby Scotts Mills. Coming back, her attention was briefly diverted, and the Land Cruiser wandered. She turned sharply to get back on course, but the car started to skid; like many 4-wheel drive vehicles, it oversteers. She overcorrected, and the car rolled.

Holly came out of it with a gash on her left arm that was closed with stitches and soon healed. Otherwise, there were no injuries to any of the kids. I looked at the wrecked car and shuddered. What if one of them hadn't buckled his seat belt? What if there had been a fifth teenager sitting in the middle where the roof caved in? What if . . ? I took a deep breath. There's no point in being mesmerized by "what if," not in fishing, and not in life. I thanked God repeatedly for the kids' protection and retrieved what few items I could from the Land Cruiser.

A wrecked car and a scared teenager were not what I wanted to come home to after a float down the John Day River. I was relieved that the children were safe. Once past that, I had to deal with such practical matters as finding a new fishing vehicle. I'd driven the Land Cruiser over 135,000 miles, much of that on rough roads in pursuit of Oregon's fish. For all the abuse the car had taken, I'd spent less than $100 on non-routine maintenance. I'd towed boats with it, toted rafts, cooked meals off its tailgate, and slept in it. We'd covered a lot of ground together, but now it was history.

For the next couple of weeks I wrangled with the insurance company, researched the pickup and sport utility markets, and selected a vehicle. Toyota had a new model of Land Cruiser but wanted twice as much money as I'd paid for my old one. That option was out. I finally settled on a Dodge 4X4 pickup with a canopy. It was not as compact as the Land Cruiser, nor could it carry as many people, but it was a good rig for me and one or two others, and it got decent gas mileage for a vehicle of its size. I hyperventilated a few times and wrote a check.

Lower Columbia River, near Astoria

This new rig's mission was to take me fishing, and on our first trip together I trailered the Klamath to the John Day boat ramp. This was a different John Day, though, than on my last outing. Oregon has two rivers by that name, and this one is near Astoria (that John Day guy got around). It is a short river, and empties into the Columbia east of Tongue Point.

It was a beautiful day in late June when I arrived. The North Pacific High was in place. It's a weather system that wards off storms, and its arrival marks the beginning of long days of hot sun and no rain.

There was a time when I didn't fish much in the spring because I figured I'd fish in the summer. This proved to be a poor strategy. When the schoolhouse doors close, it's time to do things as a family. I don't resent this. In fact, I welcome it. But there is no question that it affects my fishing. From now until Labor Day, I'd take more day trips and fewer extended jags. I'd reserved a few days in July to take advantage of the damselfly migration at Crane Prairie Reservoir, but otherwise most of my fishing would be close to home or part of a family outing.

The tide was low but had just turned when I launched the Klamath. As I motored toward the Columbia, an old wooden boat, sunken onto its side, lay exposed. Boats beguile me, especially wooden ones, and every time I pass this derelict I speculate on its age and history. I'm sure a little checking around would reveal the mystery, but then the fun would be gone.

Mid-river pilings wore a top-knot of grass tufts and willow stems. A heron stood sentinel on one, a kingfisher perched on another. Gulls stalked the mud flats looking for whatever it is gulls look for. The coastal environment was a refreshing change from the desert and Valley rivers I'd been fishing all spring. The intriguing thing was that the herons and kingfishers were a constant. Given water and fish, you'll find them most anywhere in Oregon.

My destination was a patch of water outside Lois Island. Straight out from the John Day there is a shallow passage between

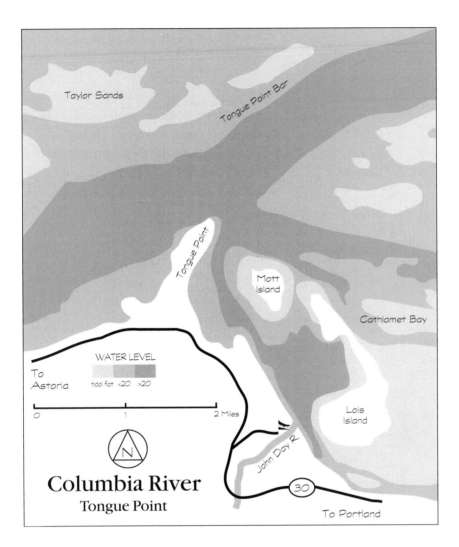

Columbia River
Tongue Point

Lois and Mott Islands, but today's minus tide left no water in that channel, so I motored west to Tongue Point, then turned east and headed upriver. It was a warm day, over 70 degrees, and only one cloud hung in the blue sky. It was long and skinny like my quarry, the white sturgeon.

Sturgeon fascinate me. They are so efficient and well-adapted to their environment that they have changed little in their 300-million year history. I'm awestruck when I consider that these fish were around when dinosaurs ruled Oregon. In fact, they were around when most of today's Oregon didn't even exist.

Not only are sturgeon ancient, they are a very strange fish. Hard, sharp little diamonds run along their back and sides. They have no backbone, just cartilage. A sturgeon's mouth is on the underside, like a shark's, and has bellows-like lips that extend to suck food off the bottom. Little barbels stick out around the snout, like on a catfish, and are used to find food. Sturgeon look and act like a piscatorial vacuum cleaner: they prowl the bottom of the river hoovering up dead stuff, such as smelt, shad, and smolts.

The lower Columbia holds two species of sturgeon: white sturgeon and green sturgeon. Whites will readily adapt to fresh water and are content to spent their lives in it. Greens, on the other hand, are more of a saltwater fish. They are migratory, and sometimes come into estuaries like the lower Columbia. At times they are present in numbers equal to white sturgeon. The peculiar thing is this: although the two species appear to have nearly identical eating habits, it is quite rare to catch a green sturgeon. Of last year's catch of 50,000 sturgeon, only a few hundred where greens. I've never met anyone who could explain why green sturgeon rarely bite on sport tackle.

When white settlers first came to Oregon, they found the lower Columbia full of sturgeon. Although excellent eating, sturgeon were considered trash fish, an obstacle in the path of salmon fishing. Still, there was some food value, and a few people fished for them. There were some huge fish out there; one was landed at Astoria that weighed over 2,000 pounds.

Sometimes when the early settlers hooked a big sturgeon, they would pull it in with a team of horses. One story tells of a man who connected with a sturgeon so big his plow horse couldn't pull it onto the beach, so he went to borrow another horse. When he returned, all that remained of his plow horse was a set of scrambling hoof prints leading into the water. There is an apochryphal sequel to this story: the next day the sturgeon left a set of horseshoes on the tideflat and a note that said, "Thanks for dinner."

Near the turn of the century, a commercial market emerged for Columbia River sturgeon. Within five years the species was on the brink of extinction. With protection they have made a comeback, but big ones are rare.

I'm not a sturgeon expert, but I enjoy fishing for them a few times each year. I always come to the same place: the lower Columbia near Tongue Point. I'm mindful of the fact that I only own small boats, and the Columbia can be brutally rough. In these lower reaches the river is governed mostly by tidal flows, and when a strong eastbound wind meets the westbound ebb, steep and dangerous waves can build up. Some areas also have sandbars and treacherous currents.

My boat is only 14-feet long, so I take great care when I'm out here. I wear a life jacket and never venture far from shore, and if the wind kicks up, I'm outta there.

This may extend my life, but it limits my fishing to just a few spots. There are some good shoals near the Washington shore and productive water upstream, but I wouldn't think of going there in my little boat. Part of my sturgeon strategy is to start early in the morning because the water is usually flat. Most afternoons the wind is blowing, and I'm back at the boat ramp.

Anchoring a small boat in deep, fast-running water is a recipe for a capsize. To avoid flipping my craft, I use a "rocking chair" anchor with a buoy retrieval system and a long anchor rope. The importance of careful anchoring in the Columbia—especially upstream where the current is strong—cannot be overemphasized.

I picked my spot in 25 feet of water off Lois Island. I let the anchor down and dropped the line in the jam cleat on the bow, then brought the loose end aft where I could release it if needed. Because it was just past slack tide, I dropped a smaller anchor off the stern. When there is some current, I dispense with the stern anchor and use a sea anchor (drogue) to steady the boat.

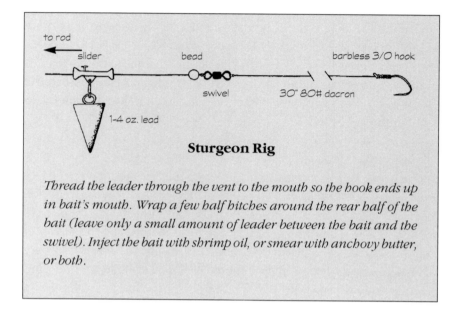

Sturgeon Rig

Thread the leader through the vent to the mouth so the hook ends up in bait's mouth. Wrap a few half hitches around the rear half of the bait (leave only a small amount of leader between the bait and the swivel). Inject the bait with shrimp oil, or smear with anchovy butter, or both.

After washing my hands thoroughly, I opened a package of frozen smelt and baited my hook. Then I injected the smelt with shrimp oil. For good measure, I covered it with anchovy butter. Sturgeon go for smell, and I believe that a mixture of strong scents provides more stimulation than a single scent. This opinion is based on gut-feelings that are backed up by no research whatsoever and reinforced by limited bait fishing experience. I have complete faith in it.

Some anglers have a misconception about sturgeon bait. They believe sturgeon go for really rotten stuff, and the smellier and rottener the better. While it's true that odor is important, sturgeon do not like rotten bait. Natural sturgeon foods are shad, spawned out smelt, salmon, carp, and lamprey eels. They also eat clams, crayfish, and even insects. They want this food barely dead (or barely alive), not old and rotten. So take a cooler and keep your bait from getting hot; it doesn't take much to ruin either frozen or fresh baitfish.

For most people, sturgeon tackle means an enormous rod that could double as a small telephone pole. I go after them with a medium-action steelhead drift rod. To some anglers this seems like using a slingshot to stop an elephant, but it is adequate tackle for most sturgeon fishing on the lower Columbia. In fact, it's better than a big stiff rod because the tip is sensitive, so I know when a bite starts. The rod is well-matched to most (but not all) fish you will hook in this part of the river.

I cast my bait about 40 feet from the boat and let it sink. Once it was on the bottom, I put the rod in its holder and cranked in enough line so there was just a little slack. Then I put on sunscreen, kicked back, and watched the freighters go by in the main channel. There were some other sturgeon anglers nearby, so I dug my binoculars out of the tackle bag and looked at them to see if they had any action. They didn't. I glassed Lois Island and spotted a deer walking along the edge.

I was daydreaming about some past or future fish when the rod tip quivered slightly. I sat up and watched it intently. It jerked again. Sturgeon maneuver fish bait so the head enters their mouth first. They can fiddle with the bait for several minutes before taking it, so patience is important. I have trouble here because my fly fisher's instinct is to set the hook the second anything touches it. Eventually the rod tugged down and stayed down. I hauled back on it.

Fifty feet of line spun off the reel, then stopped. The sturgeon kept pulling, but I pumped it up to the surface in a few minutes. A quick check revealed the fish to be about 32 inches, 10 inches too short to be a keeper. I got out the pliers, twisted the barbless hook from its mouth, and watched as it swam away.

I rebaited and soon had another bite. I lost the fish, though, when I tried to set the hook too soon. Another re-bait, another bite. This time the sturgeon stayed on. It came up more easily than the first fish, but once on the surface, it porpoised, then dove, then came back up and jumped half out of the water. But it was no bigger than the first one.

More fish came, but all were between 24 and 36 inches. No keepers. Eventually, the bite faded as the fish moved on. I decided to try a new spot and up-anchored.

"Any luck?" I asked two anglers as I passed them.

"Oh, man," one of them said in a sad voice. "A big fish just hit. He took all my line, then broke off. I've never had anything like that happen before."

Big fish are out there. Some are longer than my boat. But most of these sturgeon are small, and the typical ratio is 10 or 15 under-sized sturgeon for every keeper. This day was no exception to that rule.

I parked the boat in a shallow area farther from shore, keeping a watchful eye on the wind. Other anglers were anchored in a line along a trench. I went to the down-tide end of the line on the theory that sturgeon find their food by smell, and my position was such that any fish up-tide from me would smell everybody's bait but encounter mine first as it followed the scent trail.

It's an interesting theory, but while I soon had another fish, it didn't look like I was catching more or less than anyone else near me. I tossed out my bait again and looked at the other boats with the binoculars. In one of them, there was a guy with binoculars looking at me.

I checked my watch. It was 2:00, about time for the tide to turn. Fishing is usually best a couple of hours on either side of slack tide, but as soon as the ebb started in earnest, it would meet the afternoon wind, and I needed to seek shelter. I caught one more fish, released it, and headed closer to shore. By 3:30, I was on my way home.

You see a lot of sturgeon anglers these days. How did such a strange fish get to be so popular? Primarily because salmon and steelhead runs have been decimated by habitat loss, poor management decisions, and overharvesting. Anglers looked for something to fill the void and discovered sturgeon.

Weekend anglers aren't the only people pursuing sturgeon. Much of the pressure comes from guides and charter outfits. It didn't take the pros long to figure out where and how to catch sturgeon. When they take their clients out, there is a guarantee of lots of fish to reel in, even if few of them are keepers, and that keeps people paying to go fishing.

Heavy fishing pressure from amateurs and pros means few fish escape the slot limit. Over 90% of the catch is under the 42-inch minimum. As soon as a fish reaches 42 inches, it's chances of being caught and bonked on the head are pretty good.

Current regulations allow Oregon anglers to keep one sturgeon per day between 42 and 54 inches, and one between 54 and 66 inches. The theory behind these slots is that reproduction is not threatened because the primary spawners are too big to keep. Biologists estimate the lower Columbia sturgeon population includes 500,000 fish between three and six feet. That's a lot of fish. However, over 50,000 are "harvested" each year. Also, they grow slowly and stay in the 42-inch to 66-inch slot for almost 15 years. It doesn't take a Masters degree in statistics to figure out that a sturgeon has a slim chance of growing too big to be killed, or even of getting much past 42 inches.

It's estimated that only 1,700 fish grow past the 66-inch limit each year. Those are the fish that will continue the species. That's not a lot of room for error.

Not everyone thinks this is the right way to manage sturgeon. Some anglers have proposed increasing the minimum size to at least 48 inches. At 48 inches, they say, sturgeon start to bulk up. They have more meat and more fight. With the small sturgeon, only a third of the fish is usable, and the rest is thrown away. And the bigger fish provide much better sport. If we increased the minimum size to four feet, we'd probably have a lot better fishing.

Waiting for
the Skinny Lady

July, Crane Prairie Reservoir

Bastille Day—July 14—is a holiday I look forward to like an eight-year-old anticipates Christmas. It's not that I'm a Francophile or a supporter of revolutions. My anticipation of the date arises from damselflies.

Damselflies are beautiful little insects. A bit smaller than their dragonfly cousins, they have slender bodies (usually striped in blue and black) and graceful double wings. The nymphs are also long and slender and have an olive hue. Denizens of lakes, they live underwater for a year and swim with a wiggling motion, feeding primarily on midge larvae. By mid-July, the damselfly nymphs are mature and ready to hatch. They migrate toward above-water objects such as rocks and standing timber, crawl into the open air, and the adult emerges.

In lakes where they are plentiful, a mass migration of damselflies drives trout into a gluttonous orgy. They rip through the wiggling hoards like they might never eat again. With all these aggressive trout feeding on insects, you'd expect fly anglers to go as least as nutty as the trout. You'd be right.

Nowhere is the damselfly migration more anticipated than on Crane Prairie Reservoir. This large central Oregon lake grows, on average, the second biggest rainbow trout in the state (Klamath Lake gets first-place honors, at least at this time). Fish of five pounds or more are common, and I know one fellow who landed a 17-pounder on a fly. It takes a big biomass to grow trout of this size, and on Crane Prairie damselfly nymphs provide much of the forage.

So in mid-July, Bastille Day, I was on the road to Crane Prairie with visions of a big trout dancing across the water with my fly in its mouth. I'd fished Crane Prairie in May under windy, frigid conditions, but this trip was different. When I arrived at the Rock Creek campground in the early afternoon, the temperature was near 80, and the wind was on vacation.

The campground was busy, but I soon found a spot and eagerly queried the fly fisher who was camped next to me. He'd been there a couple of days and seemed puzzled. "Haven't seen many damselflies," he said, shaking his head. "I picked up a few fish on a Pheasant Tail. One was about five pounds, but there just haven't been many big fish caught. Maybe the migration is about to start. All this warm weather should stir 'em up."

Well, I wasn't going to let this dour guy rain on my parade. I was here at the prime time, the best part of the season for Crane Prairie's big rainbows, and nobody was going to dampen my enthusiasm. I launched the Klamath and headed into the lake.

First, I motored over to some snags. When Crane Prairie Dam was built across the upper Deschutes River, the lodgepole pines that

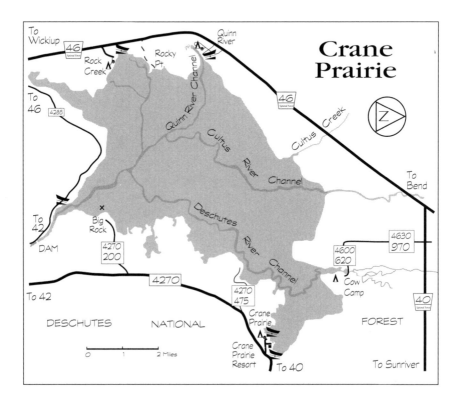

covered the flat ground were not logged. Irrigating, not fishing, was on the minds of those engineers, but when the prairie was flooded, the standing timber provided perfect habitat for trout . . . and damselflies. I examined a few snags to see if they had many nymph shucks. There were none. I looked around and spotted a few adults in the air. There weren't as many as I would expect at this time of year, but I figured the migration was just a few days late. Like the guy in the campground said, with all this warm weather they'd start moving soon enough. I just had to wait for it to happen.

No trout molested my flies that afternoon, however. Still, I kept the faith. While fixing dinner, I heard an angler in a float tube whoop and holler. His voice was muffled by distance, but I made out the words, "Biggest fish I ever caught!"

Tips for Fly Fishing Crane Prairie

Other than damselfly nymphs, the most important insects at Crane Prairie are midges, caddis, and Callibaetis mayflies (the speckled-wing quill). Sometimes a dry fly will be useful, but 90% of the time (or more) the right choice is a wet fly. Many patterns are useful, but the "must have" flies are: Olive Woolly Bugger, size 10; Leech or Woolly Bugger in both brown and black colors (size 8); Midge Pupa with gray-olive body, size 18; Flashback Pheasant Tail, sizes 14 and 16; a sparsely-tied damselfly nymph in a pattern you have confidence in (use it until the end of July).

The most useful fly line is a slow-sinking intermediate. Use a leader at least 15-feet long; 18 feet is better, and the pros go to 25 feet when there's no wind. A 3X or 2X tippet is best because of the big rainbows. Don't go to a weak tippet unless you know you're fishing over small trout; otherwise, you have to play the fish too long, which is unhealthy for them.

Write this on the back of your rod hand: "slow retrieve!" You want your fly to creep over the tops of the weeds.

Because of the wind patterns, Crane Prairie has a good, short bite around dawn, then it's slow until the wind picks up again, usually about 10:00 am. Most of the big fish cease to feed after 5:00 pm. Don't ask me why. Fishing can be good all day as long as the wind blows or if it's overcast.

When fishing that evening, I came across another fly fisher in a float tube. He was far out in Quinn Channel. "You've got a long kick back home," I said. "Do any good?"

"Two buddies of mine fished here this afternoon," he said. "They caught two; one about eight pounds, the other around ten. Caught 'em on a Beadhead Hares Ear."

I have a skepticism tempered by experience about other people's estimates of fish size (I, of course, am scrupulously honest about such things), but still, it was obvious that some big fish had been taken. I fished the Quinn channel for a while, and around sunset I had a hard grab without a hookup.

Whatever the fishing had been yesterday, it was clearly on the upswing today, and tomorrow should be dynamite. If I had patience, the fishing would come to me. I imagined the damselflies massing underwater like soldiers preparing for battle. Tomorrow the bugle would gurgle some watery notes, and there would be an all-out charge of wiggling insects. The trout would go nuts, and so would I.

The next day boats whined into the morning mist on their search for big trout. I met two returning anglers in an inflatable as I launched my own craft. "Any joy?" I asked.

"A few nice bass," one of them said. He held up a stringer of largemouth.

"See any trout?"

He shook his head. "Didn't see no trout rollin' nowhere."

There seemed to be more adult damselflies in the air. Clearly the migration and hatch were getting under way, and one more warm day would bring out the damsels. My timing for this trip couldn't have been better.

Fish still seemed hard to find, though. People, on the other hand, were in abundance. The campgrounds and waterways were filling up, mostly with fly fishers. Out-of-state license plates were common, and there was one large contingent of Japanese-American fly fishers from San Francisco. Anglers from all over the West were flocking to Crane Prairie for the big event.

I spoke to one fly fisher who'd been there the week before. "Yep," he said, "migration was just starting to roll. I had three days of good fishing, then it turned cold. They shut down like someone throwed a switch. This warm weather should get them going, though."

The thermometer topped 90 that afternoon, and the air was still and dense. Frustration was even denser, but more restless. It hung over the lake like fog and was thick enough to cut with a chainsaw. A lot of people had come here expecting the season's best fishing and were finding the opposite.

Coming onto one popular spot, I saw an angler in a rental boat with a deeply bent fly rod. He was surrounded by other boats, and all the anglers were watching him. I joined the audience. When the angler netted and released a seven pounder, everyone raised a cheer and clapped. Obviously the sight of a big fish was a rare event.

Still, the damselflies were a no show. The saying is, "It's not over till the fat lady sings." In this case, it wouldn't be over till the skinny damsel wiggled. *Patience*, I told myself. *Any day now. Sit tight and wait for the inevitable.*

Only a couple of things are inevitable, however, and the worst came very near the next morning.

The campsite next to mine was filled by two families, and while I don't mind the babble of young children, I do mind the sound of a radio in a campground—especially when it plays Elvis at midnight. I lay sleepless in my tent for a couple of hours, trying in vain to ignore the music. This was a poor strategy, and instead of falling asleep I became increasingly angry. Finally I pulled on my pants, crawled out of the tent, and—trying hard to keep the "how-could-anyone-be-so-stupid-and-inconsiderate, do-you-have-potato-peelings-for-brains?" tone out of my voice, I asked them to turn the music down. The lady of the camp acted surprised, like she had no idea someone in a tent 75 feet away could hear the radio, or if they could, that they would mind being lullabied by The King. But she turned it off.

By this time, I'd stewed long enough that I couldn't get to sleep even without Elvis. Indigestion developed, fueled by frustration with the fishing and anger at my neighbors. I tossed for hours, and it was near three in the morning before I dropped off to sleep.

In a fishing-oriented campground such as this, people wake up in two stages: the eager anglers are up at 5:00 and head for the water, and the rest of the camp sleeps until 8:30 or 9:00. I awoke between the two groups at 7:15. Nobody was up and about. After my rough night, I felt a walk would do me good. I thought about a stroll out to Rocky Point, but instead I felt a strong urge to go the other direction, up near the boat ramp.

As I walked that way, I passed a fellow sitting in a camp chair by his trailer. His face was strained, and he looked uncomfortable. "Sir," he said, "would you get the camp host for me? I don't feel well."

I went to the host's trailer and knocked on the door. A man in his late sixties appeared in a bath robe. "There's a guy over there," I said, pointing to the trailer across the way. "He says he doesn't feel well, and would you go see him."

Having delivered the message, I returned to the man in the chair. "The host is on his way," I said. "Is there anything I can do to help you?"

He shook his head. He looked worse than before. "No," he said. "I'm having chest pains."

I hightailed back to the host. "He says he's having chest pains. I think you'd better hurry."

"Be right there," the host said, slipping on his pants.

There seemed to be nothing more I could do, so I went fishing.

The damsels continued to lie low. But why? Every angler on the lake had a different theory.

"They drew down the water too low last September," said one. "Probably killed all the eggs."

"Bass ate 'em," said another. The largemouth were an illegal introduction to the lake, and most trout fisherman resent them and blame any problem on the bass.

"Wind's from the east," said one of the Japanese anglers. "It's never good here when it's an east wind."

"Been too cold," said a man in a yellow hat. "They'll come. This warm weather will do it."

But it didn't do it that day. I picked up a few small trout and diddled a half dozen 12-inch largemouths, but had none of the fishing Crane Prairie can produce when it's good.

By noon, I was worn out from chasing fish on too little sleep. I returned to camp and tried to take a nap, but the tent was like an oven. I pulled out my sleeping pad, put it on open ground, and lay down. I was almost asleep when I felt little paws running across my legs. Crane Prairie has the world's most aggressive golden-mantled ground squirrels (they look like chipmunks). I knew it was them. I was so weary, I ignored them. But they're worse than Elvis. Soon they were on my chest, and I think one was sniffing for food in my beard.

That did it; I was out of there. I packed up my stuff and headed north a few miles to Hosmer Lake. The Hosmer campground is in a ponderosa forest, so it offers more shade than Crane Prairie's thin lodgepoles. Furthermore, it is a mile off the main highway, so road noise is minimal. And there are no ground squirrels. I had a nice nap before heading back to Crane late that afternoon.

Before launching, I stopped at the campground host's trailer and asked after the man who had been so ill that morning.

"I radioed to Lava Lake," he said, "and they called an ambulance. It came from La Pine. Got here in 17 minutes."

I contemplated that drive; it takes me almost half an hour, and I'm no slow poke. The EMT crew must have been hauling.

"When they got here," the host went on, "the guy was in pain. On a scale of one to ten, he was at eight, maybe nine. The EMTs radioed for a chopper. Landed over there." He pointed. "They took him to Bend. One artery was blocked, the other collapsed. He's out of surgery now and doing fine. Another ten minutes, and he'd have been gone. Good thing you happened by when you did. He couldn't walk, and no one else was around yet."

The campgrounds on the Cascade Lakes Highway have no telephones. If there is an emergency, the hosts (usually retired people who stay there all summer) radio to the campground managers, which in this case is a private contractor at Lava Lake. They have a mobile phone and can reach the outside world. If there had been no host, or the host had not had a radio—what then?

That night and the next day the weather remained hot and calm. Trout were conspicuously absent, as were damselflies. I finally gave up and headed home. I kept my bags packed, and every couple of days I checked with Bend-area fly shops to see if the damsel migration had started. It never did. The following November I was chatting with Rick Hafele, a friend of mine who is an aquatic entomologist and fly-fishing writer. "I just read something about damselflies in a scientific journal," he said.

I was all ears. I hadn't told him about my experience at Crane Prairie that summer, about how the famous damselfly migration never happened.

"It turns out," Rick said, "that if the nymphs reach a certain instar of their growth by the summer solstice, a hormone kicks in that makes them sexually mature, and they migrate in July. If they don't reach that instar by the solstice, they won't migrate, and they won't emerge that year."

"And the growth is governed by . . ."

"By degree-days."

"So," I said, "if it's a cold spring, like we just had, they don't grow fast enough for that hormone to kick in, and they won't migrate that summer. Is that it?"

"Right."

"But they're still there, and the next July they'll migrate and the trout will go nuts."

"Could be. You never know for sure."

That was all the hope I needed. When Bastille Day comes around again, I'll be back at Crane Prairie waiting for the skinny damsel to wiggle.

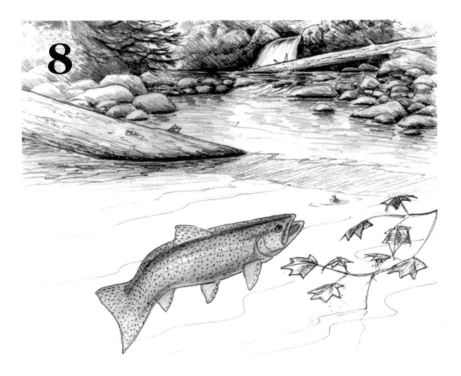

The Green Cathedral

Late July, North Coast

During the dark ages that followed the Roman Empire's collapse, Greco-Roman culture—the basis of what we now think of as European civilization—was nearly wiped out. Interested only in gold and power, the nomadic barbarians who seized control were better at destroying than building.

Christian monks and learned men sought safe havens for themselves and their ancient texts. In barren monasteries along the rocky coasts of Ireland, Scotland, and Wales, they clung by their fingernails and passed their learning to successive generations. In time, the power of the barbarians faded, and missionaries went forth to re-establish their vision of heaven.

Those ancient monks remind me of Oregon's coastal cutthroat trout.

The rivers and creeks of Oregon's coast are rocky spate streams. Heavy rains fall over steep terrain, so nutrients are flushed out to sea before they can take hold. Pick up a few stones in the Deschutes; they teem with the insects that fatten resident trout. Do the same in a coastal creek, and you'll be lucky to find one creepy-crawly for every five rocks.

It's little wonder that anadromous fish like salmon and steel-head come from these waters. There's not enough forage to feed them, so they head out to sea and grow huge off the ocean's bounty.

When salmon and steelhead smolts head for the Pacific, a poor relation stays behind: the coastal cutthroat. They linger in the tea-colored creeks and eke out a living among the boulders and along the claybanks. In some waters, especially those where falls block the upstream migration of salmon and steelhead, they even flourish.

Or they used to.

When Euro-Americans invaded the coast 150 years ago, they systematically devastated the watersheds. Tough, hard-working loggers built railroads and clearcut steep hills. Then they moved on to the next show. The denuded landscapes sloughed into creeks, and silt suffocated fish while they were still eggs. Many of those that survived were born into a land without streamside vegetation.

Waters warmed, aquatic insects perished, fish failed to repro-duce themselves. And few people cared except a handful of anglers, and most of them were interested only in the macho fish, salmon and steelhead. The humble cutthroat? Oh yeah, them.

These poor fish. They're so innocent that any dolt of an angler can catch one. Too naive to challenge ace catch-and-releasers, too small to interest meat fishermen, coastal cutthroat are one of Oregon's most under-appreciated gamefish.

On a sunny day in late July, I drove to within 20 miles of the coast, took a side road a few more miles, then parked the truck near a bridge. The climb down the bank netted only one small scratch from blackberry vines—a better than average journey.

The creek flowed dark and tannic-brown. I waded in, worked my way to a pool, and cast sidearm and downstream so the Elk Hair Caddis would drop under an overhanging alder. The fly drifted about five feet before a tiny dimple almost sucked it under. Another two feet, and down it went. I set the hook like I was expecting one of Crane Prairie's ten-pound rainbows. A four-incher flew out of the water and landed at my knee cap.

In his brilliant book *The Habit of Rivers*, Ted Leeson calls these little guys "launchers," for reasons that are obvious to anyone who's hooked one while expecting larger fare. The coastal creeks and rivers have many small fish. Some are salmon and steelhead smolts, and others are cutthroat, such as this youngster. I reminded myself of where I was, and when the next fish took my fly, I gently tightened on it. A six-inch trout bounced up to my hand. A few more casts brought another fish about the same size.

You don't fish these waters for trophies. There was a time when many of the coastal headwaters held cutthroat in the 20-24 inch range, but—bless their gullible hearts—they were soon fished out. Between habitat destruction and fishing pressure, they have not been replaced. The average catch here is five to seven inches long, and anything over ten inches is a lunker.

I continued downstream, flipping my fly under tree branches as I went. The best places to find cutthroat are in deep pools with overhanging branches and a gentle current (not slack water), near rocks, at the heads of riffles, and next to shore where a moderate current flows through water that is knee-deep or more.

In one slow-moving pool, the spreading rings of a rise appeared ten feet from my fly. I carefully lifted the Elk Hair from the water and stopped wading. The fish rose again, and this time I saw its sides. I guessed at an eight-incher (wow!) and cast toward it. The fly floated over the trout; nothing happened. Another cast, but this time there was a rise. I tightened on water, not fish.

When you have a rise but no hookup, the solid bet is you were refused: at the last second the trout rejected the fly and turned away from it. I tied on a smaller fly, a size 16 Adams. The fish took it and was quickly released.

A step at a time, I worked downstream, exploring the nooks and niches of the creek. Alder branches reached up from both banks and met in the middle. The effect was like a gothic arch with the point over the stream. Above the forest canopy, the sky was blue and the sun strong and harsh, but under the alders the leaf-filtered light was luminous but not bright, soft and without shadows.

The medieval cathedrals of Europe are like this: narrow naves and transepts with high, vaulted roofs buttressed by stone; sunlight softened and colored by stained glass. I once had a college professor who proclaimed himself an atheist, but he admitted that when he first toured the great gothic cathedrals he was awestruck. Even he was impressed by the sense of reverence embodied in stone and glass.

When fishing the green cathedrals of Oregon's coastal streams, I've sometimes wondered if some of those 13th-century architects were anglers. Walking the bed of a rippling stream in medieval England or France or Germany, they would have seen something not unlike what I see here: thick evergreens buttressing deciduous trees that crowd the creek; branches curving upward like the ribs of a vaulted nave, sunlight defused by leaves translucent as colored glass. Could a day on a trout stream have been the inspiration for Chartres?

I reversed direction and pushed upstream, looking for more good water. In a few places I could walk the bank, but most of the time I slogged through water that seldom reached above my thighs.

At one pool I spotted an orange shape on the bottom. When I touched it with my boot, it shot backwards four feet and settled on the bottom again. Crayfish. Coastal creeks are full of them, and they are forage for herons and sometimes for fish. Crayfish always travel backwards, and I've often wondered if they ever hit anything. I've never seen one carom off a rock. How do they avoid it? Do their stalk-mounted eyes see in all directions? Another crayfish mystery: why are they orange? They're hardly camouflaged. Are those little claws enough of a threat that they can use bright coloration to say, "Back off buster!"

When I fish these creeks I seem to come back with more questions than I start with.

A few more cutthroat came to my fly before I left the creek and moved on to search for another stream I'd heard about. I followed the map in the DeLorme atlas and found the access road. It was blocked by a heavy yellow gate. A big "Logging in Process. No Trespassing" sign hung from the top rail.

I checked the maps and found another way in. For the next hour I bumped over dirt roads, checked map and compass, felt my way, and finally was blocked by a downed tree. Since I had no chainsaw in the truck, this was the end of the road, so I backed up to a turn-around and headed home.

Cutthroat anglers are frequently frustrated in their efforts to find good water. Habitat loss, blocked roads, and stream closures have shrunk what was once an abundant fishery into just a few enclaves. Trial and error are the only ways to find a decent creek, so you have to feel that exploration is part of the experience. And when you stumble onto a good stream, you release all the trout, and keep your mouth shut.

Fishing in Oregon gives some good guidelines and starting points. I always carry a copy in my truck, as well as keep one at home. The DeLorme atlas is another excellent tool. This book has topographic maps for the entire state, and while I often wish the scale were bigger, it's adequate for most situations. I've tried the Metzger county maps but find them cluttered and hard to read, so I stick with DeLorme most of the time.

Once you find a suitable stream, access is the next obstacle. Much of the coastal land is privately owned, mostly by large timber companies. Recent decades have brought such a dread of lawsuits that property owners have shut the public out of their lands. Many good cutthroat streams are behind a locked gate and a phalanx of "No Trespassing" signs. I find this aggravating, yet understandable. It only takes an aggressive lawyer and a few bozo clients to mess things up for the rest of us. ("Your honor, the timber company was obviously negligent for not telling my poor client he would be hurt if a 120-foot tree landed on his head.")

And many non-corporate property owners only have to look around at the litter many visitors scatter about—everything from styrofoam worm cups to condoms—to say "stay out."

Once a cutthroat angler has found a stream and a way to get to it, the next challenge is to get from one pool to the next. The banks of these creeks are a tangle of alders, vine maples, and blackberries. Usually it's impossible to make any progress unless you stay in the streambed, but many creeks have surprisingly deep pools, and hip boots won't get you through them. For this reason, I either wear chest waders or, if it's summer, I wade wet. When wet wading, I slip on a pair of dark green synthetic pants made for whitewater rafters. These provide a measure of camouflage and, more to the point, keep the blackberries from shredding my legs. I wear my studded wading boots over a pair of knee-high polypropylene socks which have warmth even when they are wet. I also keep a change of clothes in the truck because when you wade the creeks, slips and duckings are not unknown.

Because mobility is essential when fishing small streams, it's best to stay unencumbered. That's why I keep my gear simple—a few flies, floatant, a spool of tippet material, nippers, forceps, pocket knife, toilet paper in a ziplock bag, maybe a candy bar or a sandwich. If it doesn't fit into my shirt pockets or a small shoulder bag, it doesn't go.

A short, lightweight rod makes the best tool. I use a four-weight fly rod I built from a fiberglass blank. Although it started life seven-and-a-half feet long, an unfortunate accident reduced it to a seven footer. I chose fiberglass because it loads better when there isn't much line past the rod tip, and long casts are seldom necessary for this kind of fishing.

On these creeks I use a seven-foot leader tapered to 5X and a double-taper floating line. While I prefer dry flies, I don't fish with them exclusively. Many of the bigger fish are in deep pools, and a wet fly or nymph can be the best way to approach them. Most anglers look at a small stream and think only in terms of dry flies, but even cutthroat often prefer a subsurface fly to a dry.

My small stream fly box has these standard patterns: Tan Elk Hair Caddis, Parachute Adams, and Pheasant Tail nymphs, all in sizes 14, 16, and 18; Griffiths Gnat and some kind of midge pupa in sizes 18 and 20; size 10 Olive Woolly Bugger.

I made another trip to the coastal creeks in late July. This time I was a little farther south and had company. Dave Hughes, my companion on the John Day, sat in the truck's right-hand seat reading the map and issuing directions. The suspicions I'd had on the John Day about Dave and his Japanese friend Masako Tani proved correct. Next week Masako would jet to Oregon and marry Dave. With some effort, I avoided making end-of-bachelorhood jokes.

"So where's this river?" I asked Dave.

Dave looked around and rubbed his chin, then waved his hand forward. "Keep going. I think it's over that next ridge."

Dave is a master of these coastal creeks and wrote eloquently about them in his book *An Angler's Astoria*. He'd heard of a good piece of water that neither of us had tried, so we searched for it together. For two hours we bounced along rough roads, taking shortcuts that added miles to the trip but seeing some nice scenery. Eventually we arrived at the sought-after stream, a north fork of a north fork of a north coast river.

"Look at that," I said, eyeing an ODFW sign nailed to a tree. "They got the dates reversed." The sign said fishing was allowed from May 27 to June 15. "It should be the other way around, open June 15 to May 27. They probably close it for a few weeks so smolts can escape. I'd think the smolts would have gone out a few weeks earlier, though."

Dave looked pensive, like he'd just remembered he'd left the water running at home. "Maybe they mean it. Here's another sign, and it says the same thing. We'd better check the regs."

I pulled a copy of the angling regulations from my bag and looked up the entry for this river. I read it, then read it again, and finally announced, "They mean it. The river is open three weeks a year. Why do they even bother? Why don't they just close it down?

"You know," Dave began slowly, "I think you and I are partly responsible for this. I think Oregon Trout pushed for this closure to protect wild salmon and steelhead." Dave founded Oregon Trout, the state's largest fish conservation group, and I edit the newsletter. So yes, this was probably our fault, and we deserved it.

"I suppose we could have checked out the regs before we drove over here," I said.

Dave shook his head. "Too easy," he said. "Much too easy."

We looked up nearby creeks and tributaries. All were closed. We checked the atlas to see what else we could reach and settled on a creek somewhat to the north.

Before World War II, Dave's father had fished this creek, but found poor pickings because it was still recovering from its first logging. In the 1960s, though, the trees reached maturity and fishing became superb.

Dave fished the creek often, sometimes camping overnight. "One day," he said, "I caught 30 trout on one fly, then 10 on another. And those were just the fish over eight inches. Some of them were 13 or 14 inches long, which is pretty good for coastal cutthroat."

When Dave returned from Viet Nam, he found his favorite creek under siege. A logging road had been punched through, and harvest begun. Soon, the entire watershed was logged. "It was decimated," Dave said. "They left buffer trees along the creek bed, as the law required, but they were junk alder. When the first storm came off the coast, all the trees blew over and fell into the stream. For three or four years, you couldn't even walk the creekbed." Even after the alders rotted out, he still couldn't wade in the creek because the silt was so thick and slippery.

Without overhead cover, the few struggling cutthroat were exposed to overhead predators, and the water temperature soared. Without cold water, the insect base plummeted. "I went in one day," Dave said, "and picked huckleberries. Along the way, I cut down hemlock branches with a machete and put them over deep holes and other places trout might hide. I don't know if it did any good, but it made me feel better."

Fish were still there, but not little ones. This was a bad sign; natural reproduction had ceased. Then the Oregon Department of Fish and Wildlife decided the creek would be good salmon rearing habitat, so they planted coho fry. After a couple of years, ODFW gave up on the coho venture. In the meantime, the coho fry out-competed the cutthroat for the creek's meager forage. Hardly any of the native fish were left. "I come back here once every year or two," Dave said. "Just to see how it's doing. It's not doing well."

The really sad thing is that this creek's history is not unique. A similar story could be told about nearly every creek and river in the Coast Range.

Our visit was to be one of Dave's biennial checkups. I'd never been here before, so I had no basis of comparison. It looked good. The young third-growth firs were now 20 feet high, and the canopy over the creek was beginning to close. The water was clear and cold. Fish could live here, I thought.

I watched Dave rig a beautiful seven-foot, five-strip cane rod hand-crafted for him by Dean Jones of Portland.

"I'd be scared to death to take a rod like that on a little creek," I said. "First trip out, I'd probably fall and break it."

"I've noticed you're not very coordinated," Dave said.

"You've been watching my casting."

"I've watched you fall in the river when you were standing still and hanging onto the boat. Are you sure this creek is open?"

"I checked three times."

We walked downstream along the road, then cut to the creek, planning to fish our way back to the truck. Dave was rigged with a small nymph and a yarn indicator. I tied on an Adams dry fly. We leapfrogged each other up the creek, kneeling low as we reached each pool, exploring boulders and runs, dropping flies into plunge pools. Nothing molested our flies, and Dave was becoming discouraged. It looked like this stream would never be resurrected, at least not in our lifetimes.

"Do you think someone's been here before us?" I said.

Dave pointed his rod at a rock. "Yes, and he's a better fisherman than you or me."

I looked at the rock. Two wet footprints splayed across it. "No wonder. Poor little cutts don't want to show themselves."

Coming around the next bend, we came upon the angler we'd been following for an hour: a great blue heron that lifted off a rock and flew upstream when we arrived.

In the next pool, Dave's nymph found its way into the mouth of a 10-inch cutthroat, and a bit later one grabbed my Adams. After two hours of fishing, those were the only two trout we hooked. There were no small fish, no signs of a future.

Back at the truck, Dave said, "Maybe in another 10 or 15 years, it will be good again. But once it recovers, how long before the loggers come back?"

On the other hand, if we let the green cathedrals of the coast rebuild themselves, how long before missionary cutthroat go forth and spread a vision of heaven in which we all can rejoice?

9

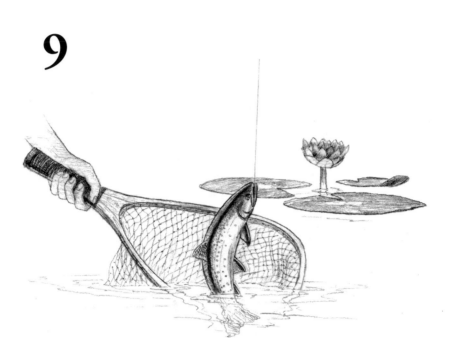

Kid Fishing

August, Quinn Meadow Horsecamp

During breakfast, Alex asked if he could please go fishing today. Pleading dripped from his voice like the syrup that ran off his pancakes. Alex had been fishing a couple of times in his eight years on planet Earth, but he'd never caught anything. I'd already put him off forever (two days), but the time was right, so I agreed: today was the day.

Alex belongs to a family in my daughter's 4-H group. Three-dozen of us were camped for a week at the Quinn Meadow horse camp, a fine Forest Service facility near the Cascade Lakes Highway. While horseback riding was the primary purpose of our visit, we were very close to some excellent fishing. It would have been a sin not to take advantage of the opportunities that surrounded us, and I just happened to pack a few fishing rods along with the horse gear.

I asked Keiko if she wanted to come with Alex and me. Keiko is a 15-year old Japanese girl who was staying with us for three weeks. She listened to my explanation of what we were going to do and grasped the meaning without too many trips to the English-Japanese dictionary. So the three of us climbed into the truck and headed for Lava Lake.

I like taking kids fishing, and I've done it enough times to realize that kid fishing is not the same as adult fishing. The biggest difference is that when you take a child, it's their trip. The focus has to be on the youngsters, and your only role is to keep them safe and happy and to help them catch fish. If you figure you're going to go fishing and let a kid tag along and put a line in the water while you do your thing, there will be two very frustrated people at the end of the day.

Time does odd things to an adult's memory. I fished a lot as a child, but if I recall those long summer days of dangling worms off docks, I'm liable to put an adult spin on it and see a small version of my grownup self: eager, attentive, ready to learn, analyzing the situation carefully, taking good care of my tackle.

But if I hold memory up to the hard light of reality, a different picture emerges: when I was eight, nine, ten years old, fishing—like everything else—was a game. My friends and I would toss our worms into Lake Washington and watch our cork bobbers for a long time (probably ten minutes). If there was no immediate action, we'd leave the lines in the water and plop concrete blocks on top of the rods. Then we'd skylark around on shore, walking on logs, throwing rocks, playing cowboys or tag. Every 15 minutes or so one of us would trot out to the dock to see if a suicidal perch had swallowed the hook and was hanging half-dead at the end of the line.

We had no sense of ethics and little patience. We abused our tackle and the fish, and had only the barest knowledge of angling.

Further, we were so ignorant that we didn't know how little we knew, and we were ill-inclined to learn more.

A strong interest in becoming a better angler came sometime after my twelve birthday, and I think it's the same for most kids. Any younger, and fishing is a fun thing to do outside, an activity that puts you in touch with the outdoors and with friends or parents. It's an opportunity to kill time, to explore new ground, and maybe have an adventure. But it quickly becomes tedious if you have to "learn stuff" or "do things the right way."

Before I take a child fishing, I try to spend a few minutes reminding myself what it is was like to be eight years old. Once I'm in touch with that, I'm ready to go.

Lava Lake

Lava Lake covers about 400 acres and has stunning views of South Sister, Mt. Bachelor, and Broken Top. The fish are stocked rainbows with a few brook trout. Because the lake has decent forage, the trout grow well, and many survive the winter. The typical fish is 14-16 inches, and bigger ones—up to four or five pounds—are out there.

I parked the truck in the gravel lot and went into the old log lodge to rent a boat. "How's the fishing?" I asked Joann Frazee. Joann and her husband not only run Lava Lake Resort, they own High Lakes Contractors and take care of dozens of Forest Service campgrounds. Joann is a rarity among resort owners: if I ask her how the fishing is, I get an honest answer. More than once she's told me the fishing was "poor, very poor." How many resort owners will admit that?

Today she told me it was "pretty good," and I grew suddenly optimistic about this expedition.

"How long do you want the boat?" she asked.

"A couple of hours." I looked at my neophyte anglers. "That should be enough."

I distributed life jackets, fishing tackle, and a couple of sodas between them, and we headed for the rental boat. The wind was

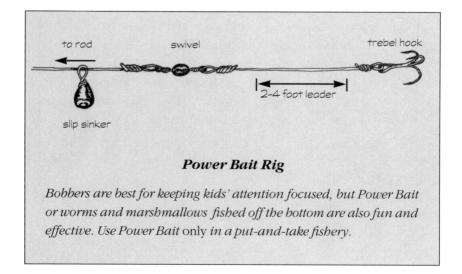

Power Bait Rig

Bobbers are best for keeping kids' attention focused, but Power Bait or worms and marshmallows fished off the bottom are also fun and effective. Use Power Bait only in a put-and-take fishery.

blowing about 15 miles an hour from the north, and it was choppy at the south end of the lake where the resort is located. As we motored out, spray arced from under the boat, and some blew back in our faces. The kids huddled in their jackets. Nothing kills a kid-trip faster than cold and damp, so I headed for the sheltered north end of the lake. Once we were there, Keiko and Alex soon warmed up and emerged from their jackets.

I put out our bow and stern anchors so we wouldn't swing— you can't still-fish from a boat that isn't still—and started to rig the tackle. I'd brought my ultralight spinning rod, and Alex's mother had sent along two fishing rods. When I pulled line off the loaner rods it hung in stiff coils, like a telephone cord. The gear was useless. I finished rigging the rods anyway so each kid would have something to hang onto, then I set up my ultralight.

The technique of the day was still-fishing with Power Bait. Power Bait is a chemical concoction with awesome attractive powers. It comes in several colors not found in nature, and some varieties sink while others float. I was using the floating kind. The right way to fish with this stuff is to put a sliding pendant sinker on the main line, then attach a swivel and leader. The bait is molded onto a treble hook. When cast, the sinker rests on the bottom and the bait floats above it. Ideally, the bait should be just above the tops of the weeds because that is where the trout spend most of their time. When a fish picks up the bait, the line slides through the sinker, and the fish doesn't feel any weight or resistance.

This method of bait fishing is what I call "fishing from the bottom up." Its converse, "fishing from the top down" uses a float or bobber to suspend the bait. Today we were anchored in 25 feet of water, and the fish were near the bottom, so fishing from the bottom up was the best approach.

It wasn't long before there was some action. The line on my rod began to move. "Here's a fish," I said, and handed the rod to Keiko. "Reel it in."

I don't think she knew what "reel" meant, and there was no time to look it up in the dictionary. I cranked the handle a couple of times, and she got the idea. Alex leaned over the side of the boat and watched the silvery trout twist up through the water. I handed him the net, and he took a swipe at the trout like the net was a racket and the fish was a tennis ball. He hit the trout hard but didn't knock it off the line. One thing about Power Bait: fish inhale it, so unless the trout is so big that it will break off (not a problem in this case), it's hooked for life.

"Just hold the net still," I told Alex. "Let Keiko bring the fish to it. When the trout is over the net, bring it up. Not too fast."

He tried it again. The net still wiggled some (try getting an eight-year old boy to hold anything still for more than three microseconds), but the trout fell into it.

I took the fish from the net, and turning my back to Keiko and Alex, I broke its neck. "There's one for breakfast," I said as I put the trout down. The kids admired its pretty colors while I re-baited and cast out again. "Your turn, Alex." I said. "The next fish is yours."

Ten minutes later, the line started to move around. "Fish on, Alex," I said. Alex, whose attention seemed to be fixed on another boat, suddenly became alert and stared at the line.

"Wow," he said. He grabbed the rod and started reeling in as fast as he could.

"Slow down. It'll stay on."

Hints for Fishing with Kids under 12

Keep them warm and dry; if the weather's bad, don't go.
If they're in a boat, they wear a life jacket. Period.
For safety, go to lakes, not rivers.
Don't take too many kids (two, maybe three, per adult).
Two hours is the limit for most youngsters.
Forget fishing yourself and concentrate on helping the kids.
Go to a put-and-take fishery with a high chance of success.
Give everybody something to do.
Guide, but don't criticize.
Patience.
Keep it simple.
*Prop up the rods; otherwise they'll never keep them still
    enough to catch a fish.*
If they want to quit after an hour, let them.
*Feed them and be sure they use the toilet before they
    get in the boat.*
*See Fishing in Oregon for a list of good places to take
    kids fishing.*

Keiko wielded the net, and another fish came into the boat.

After the first two trout, we had no more bites for fifteen minutes. Alex saw a fish landed in another boat. "Let's go over there," he said, like he'd just figured out where the lake stored all its trout.

"I've been watching them," I said. "We've caught more fish than they have. Besides, would you like it if everybody anchored next to you when you were catching fish?"

"Oh."

I moved the boat a couple of hundred feet and put the lines out again. By this time, I had no faith in the loaner rods with their kinked-up line and was relying exclusively on my ultralight. Keiko and Alex took turns with it, and whoever didn't have the rod would net the fish.

I knew Alex was having a good time, and it looked like Keiko was, too. When it was her turn, she watched the rod carefully, and when a fish was on, she eagerly reeled it in.

Alex kept looking around at the other boats. "Ooh," he said. "They got a big one over there! Let's move the boat to where they are."

I looked at the other boat. They were netting a trout no bigger than the one we had just landed. "I think we're doing fine here," I said.

A few minutes later this conversation was repeated as a boat on the other side of us landed a fish. "Hang tight, kid," I told Alex. "We're catching as many as anybody. And if you'll pay attention to your line, you'll notice it has a fish on it."

He looked at the line as it started to zig-zag through the water. "Wow!" he said. "Another one!"

After two hours of fishing, we reeled up and headed back to the resort. We had seven fish in the boat, three for Alex and four for Keiko. At camp, I snapped photos of Alex and Keiko holding their catch, then I cleaned the fish.

When fishing with kids, I usually gut the fish when they're not around. I adopted this philosophy some years ago after I took my ten-year old nephew and his friend fishing in Puget Sound. My nephew's friend watched as guts oozed out of a bug-eyed, three-pound rockfish I was eviscerating. "Eeww!" he said. "I wonder what God's thinking." Since then, I've left fish cleaning as a lesson for later.

Back at camp, there were more photos. Alex showed his fish to other kids in the group and the next morning he ate one for breakfast. By afternoon he was pulling on his mom's sleave, insistent as a tea kettle at full boil: "Please can I go fishing again?"

I love making a convert.

Listening to the Wind

August

When I was a boy, my only transportation was a bicycle, and my angling was mostly confined to neighborhood docks along Lake Washington. When I reached the age of sixteen and became an adult (or so I thought), I procured a driver's license, and a new world of fishing opened up to me. Mobility meant freedom to fish where I wanted, and the mountain lakes of the Cascades became my goal.

In college I met John Hill, a like-minded angler and backpacker, and we often trekked into Washington's Cascades and fished the high lakes. We were at the peak of youthful impatience and often pressed the season. I remember one lake we hiked to in late May. Snow covered its banks, and only half the lake was ice-fee. Across the lake from our campsite, a cliff rose 3,000 feet almost straight up. As I fished a little patch of open water, avalanches roared down the sides of the mountain every five minutes.

Sometimes John and I were not so lucky. On our first trip or two of the season, we usually found the lakes frozen solid. After a while, we figured out that no matter how much we willed it otherwise, water would stay frozen until it wanted to thaw. In most cases, that meant June or even July. And the thaw was followed by a month of mosquitoes thick enough to darken the sun.

In August and September, however, the lakes were perfect: clear of snow, ice, and most biting pests. Then October would arrive and the weather would turn iffy, even dangerous, and we stayed away. But for two glorious months the lakes were there to be enjoyed, and we would load up our packs and head for the mountains.

My fishing gear was simple: a four-piece spinning rod I'd built myself, a Mitchell 304 reel (paid for with paper route money), four-pound line, and a small plastic box that fit in my shirt pocket. This box held hooks, split shot, float, and a few spinners. A jar of salmon eggs provided bait and went into a pocket of my Levis.

We'd set up a simple camp with a lean-to shelter made from a sheet of plastic tarp, and spend most of the day fishing. Time makes memory a liar, and I realize my recollections of these trips are too sunny: blue skies, eager fish, good food. But what I remember most—and I know memory plays no con games here—is the wind.

Some people who live in cities describe the woods as silent. Hogwash. The mountains and forests are full of sounds. They're just different and less annoying than what you hear in town. The caw of crows, the yap of a jay, the skitter of squirrels across a log, the buzz of flies, a marmot's whistle—the woods are never quiet. And providing a background harmony to all other sounds, is the rush of the wind in the evergreens.

When John Hill and I backpacked into the Cascades, our standard practice was to fish hard in the mornings and evenings because that's when the air was still. After lunch, I'd scrunch up a wool shirt to use as a pillow, then stretch out on the brown dirt and listen to the wind.

Even a gentle breeze makes branches sway and trunks nod. Needles vibrate slightly, moving the air just enough so the combined shimmer of billions and billions of them translates the invisible wind into something human sense can appreciate. The wind rises and falls, giving the trees rhythm and harmony, tempo and volume. It is a symphony without melody, but whose harmonies can touch a listening soul.

The wind sounds different on the east slope of the Cascades than on the west slope. Firs dominate the wetter side of the mountains, while the arid east is home to ponderosa pines. The firs are more numerous, but their needles are smaller. This gives the west side a louder song that is softer in tone. In pine country, the trees *wooosh* more. And a mixture of evergreens and deciduous trees has an even different sound, especially in fall when dry leaves rattle.

Every forest has its sounds, and you can't hear them in a crowd or near a highway. You have to leave the baggage of the modern world behind and head into the hills. There, a few miles from distraction, even city-dulled ears can hear the trees give voice to the wind.

John's and my trips to the mountain lakes came to an end. The maturity that brought mobility also brought education, employment, responsibility. John was the first to go. He graduated, took a job downstate, and we lost touch. A year later, I accepted a position with a California company in the Bay Area. It started as a temporary stay but lasted eight years. I tried hiking and fishing in the Sierras, but never got into it—too many people, too far to go, and above all too arid, rocky, and treeless for a kid who grew up with creeks, lakes, and thick evergreen forests in his backyard.

By the time I returned to the Northwest, I had a wife, a child (and the prospect of another), and was deep in the throes of remodeling an old house. It was a period in which fishing was all but elbowed from my life.

When angling again became a major activity for me, I returned to the lakes, but now they were mostly ones that had roads to their shores. I admit that schlepping a 50-pound pack up a steep trail doesn't have the appeal it once did.

But the high lakes still beckon, and there are other ways to get there. With age has come a certain finesse for avoiding the sweat and muscle approaches of youth. Many lakes are an easy one-day hike, and I can build a pretty good case that an eight-mile round trip with a day pack is less work than packing all your gear four miles, staying the night, then packing it out again the next day.

Near the Cascade Lakes Highway

It was a hot day in August when I arrived at the trail head on the east side of the Cascades. I was headed for a small lake that I had visited on horseback the year before but hadn't fished. *Fishing in Oregon* said the lake had "fair fishing for 7-10 inch brook trout." That's a common description for most mountain lakes. Naturally barren, they are stocked with either brook trout, rainbows, or cutthroat trout, and of these the brook trout best survive the harsh climate.

The water is seldom productive, and the growing season is short, so the trout rarely grow to any size. But there are a few exceptions: some high lakes grow brookies up to 15 inches and more. The one I was headed for, however, was more typical. I don't visit these lakes to find trophies. I go for the experience of being in the high country, for the wildness—and to listen to the wind.

I stocked the pockets of my float tube with fishing gear and a few essentials, snapped the shoulder straps to it, and hoisted it up. The rod went in one hand, the fins in the other, and a camera hung from my neck. My feet were clad with the rubber-soled neoprene booties I wear when I'm float-tubing. They are not something I like to hike in very far, but today's walk was less than two miles, and they would be adequate.

Less than an hour later I arrived at a typical mountain lake of about 40 acres. The bottom was a mix of cobbles and silt, and evergreens grew to the edges. A few trees had fallen in, so near the shore there was an underwater tangle of limbs and trunks that made good fish habitat. A few trout rose, probably sipping midges. The rise forms were not large, as *Fishing in Oregon* had predicted.

I figured the fish would keep a few minutes, so I propped the tube against a log, leaned against it and closed my eyes while the wind filled my ears. When I awoke 30 minutes later, the fish were still rising, and I felt refreshed enough to chase after them.

Launching a float tube at a mountain lake can sometimes be a problem. Shorelines are often steep and covered with downed trees, and this lake was no exception. Eventually I accomplished the task and set forth on a circumnavigation, casting and trolling a small fly around the lake. Fishing proved no better nor worse than expected, and the trout no bigger than predicted. An hour before sunset I was packed up and ready to head down the trail.

This is the time I miss backpacking. There is almost always a midge hatch at dusk, and that is when trout often do their most active feeding of the day. But I was alone and lightly equipped, and felt cautious about walking out alone in the dark on an unfamiliar trail. I didn't mind. I'd found what I'd come for: scenery, a pleasant solitary kick around a blue-green lake, a few brookies, and above all, a good earful of the wind in the trees.

I hoofed my way down the trail humming Gilbert and Sullivan's *When I was a Lad*, and didn't feel the least bit ironic about it.

11

Blood Lust

August, Green Peter Reservoir

There was a time when fishing meant only one thing: meat on the table. Eventually, or maybe even from the get-go, hunter-man and hunter-woman decided the pursuit of finny critters was fun, and fishing was regarded as enjoyable. But the dinner plate was still the ultimate destination of the quarry. This attitude persisted until recent times. Unless you were one of the privileged few, the wheel of fortune was lubricated by sweat, and fishing only for plea-sure was regarded as an egregious violation of the Protestant work ethic.

In recent decades, however, the Oregon country has seen great prosperity. Food is cheap enough that it's hard to justify fishing as a means of feeding a family; you can buy a lot of chicken and sausage with what most anglers plunk down for tackle, boats, and gas. At the same time, foodfish staples, such as salmon, have declined in numbers even as the human population has soared. It's becoming tougher and tougher to justify killing a fish.

For these reasons, catch-and-release has become part of the ethic of many Oregon anglers, and the movement to pure sport has strong momentum. I'm an advocate of catch-and-release fishing, especially for wild, native species. I enjoy eating fish, but I have more fun catching them, so I release 95% of what comes to my hand.

But no matter how Ivory-soap pure I try to be, I cannot dodge the fact that fishing has its roots in blood.

I can argue with anybody about why we need to conserve fish, about how a careful catch-and-release angler does little harm to the resource, about how quickly the fish recover, how they have few nerves in their mouths and so feel little pain, and that it's the catch-and-release people that habitually take better care of the rivers and lakes and all that dwells in them.

But sometimes I just want to kill something and eat it.

When ancient instincts bubble up from the psychic sump, I restrict myself to certain bodies of water and certain species of fish: hatchery chinook on the Willamette; stocked rainbows in lakes that would otherwise be barren; panfish in waters where they are plentiful.

However, there is one fish that bears the brunt of my atavistic urges: kokanee.

Kokanee are landlocked sockeye salmon. They are native to several lakes in Oregon where geological upheavals cut off the anadromous fishes' path to the ocean. Trapped sockeyes adapted to the fresh water environment, and as long as they have access to running water, they will spawn and perpetuate themselves. Like all Pacific salmon, they die after spawning.

It took a while for kokanee to catch on as a gamefish. Because they feed almost entirely on zooplankton—microscopic animals—catching them requires special techniques that take into account a few quirks of the kokanee mind. Many anglers now know enough to catch a few kokanee, and the species has become a popular gamefish. I enjoy a little kokanee fishing now and then, and I rarely release one. There are two reasons I keep them: first, in most lakes, kokanee were originally derived from hatchery stock and are quite plentiful, so much so that it does little harm and often much good to remove them from waters in which their fecundity outstrips the lake's planktonic productivity; second, they taste really good.

When the me-kill-fish, me-eat-fish urge came on me in August, I trailed the Klamath up to Green Peter Reservoir, an impoundment of the Middle Santiam River near Sweet Home.

The reservoir's name has prompted many rude speculations about its origins. I'm going to throw etymological cold water on all of them. The word "peter" is derived from the Greek "petros," which means rock. Being cultured people with a knowledge of classical languages, early surveyors sometimes used the word to describe a rocky, treeless outcropping or summit. There is a barren, green-hued knob near here, and it leant its name to the reservoir. So let's hear no more guffaws or locker-room jokes about what happens to your body if you eat the fish.

I arrived at Green Peter near evening. I'd never been to the lake before, but a friend had told me about some good kokanee fishing he'd had in spring, so I came to explore. I wandered around the roads that circle the lake and eventually stumbled on a boat ramp at Thistle Creek.

While I got ready to launch, a big guy with a broad, freckled face and a red beard drove up on an ATV. Two girls, about eight or ten years old, sat behind him. I had no idea where the kokanee would be found in Green Peter, so I thought I'd see if he knew.

"Have you done any fishing?" I asked.

"Nah," he said. "We brought some poles, but we're spending

too much time playing with other toys."

"Where do people usually fish here?"

He swept a thick arm from one end of the lake to the other. "I've seen them everywhere."

Armed with no more information than I arrived with, I launched and set forth. Only one other boat was on my part of the lake, and the anglers in it wouldn't admit to having caught any fish. A few blips showed up on my locator screen, mostly around 55 feet. I rigged up, lowered the downrigger to that depth, and trolled near an island. Before sunset, I hooked one fish and brought it to the boat. This is the point at which I usually reach down with my forceps, gently remove the hook, and watch with pleasure as the fish swims away.

Not on this trip.

I netted the kokanee, stuck my finger in its mouth, and bent back its head. There was a "crunch," as its neck broke, and it quivered for a couple of seconds before growing still. Blood ran from its gills, down its sides, and onto the bottom of the boat. I tossed the kokanee in the cooler for tomorrow's lunch and rinsed the blood from my hands.

The next morning I was on the lake at daybreak. Mist rose from the water, and yellow-tinged clouds hung about the mountains to the east. There was no morning chill, which promised a warm afternoon. A weak breeze gave the lake just enough chop to make for good fishing.

Five boats trolled along the opposite shore, but no nets flashed. I slowed my boat and turned on the locator. It marked a few fish, but nothing like a school. I set my downrigger to 55 feet, the depth at which I'd caught last night's kokanee. I'd use that as a starting point and raise and lower the downrigger until fish started grabbing my lure.

Once you've positioned yourself on a lake, there are four elements involved in kokanee fishing: lure, scent, trolling speed, and depth. The first three are easily dealt with: I use a small spoon, such as a

Triple Teaser, with a single kernel of white corn on the hook point, and troll at a very slow speed. The fourth element—depth—is where most kokanee anglers blow it.

Because kokanee feed on plankton, they are found at the levels at which plankton is concentrated. In general, the warmer the lake, the deeper the plankton, and late in the season fish can be found pretty far down—often between 50 and 80 feet. The traditional way of fishing that deep is to use a heavy lead weight or lead-core line. With that kind of rig, several factors determine the depth your lure will reach: trolling speed, wind, amount of lead, thickness of line, etc. With so many variables, hitting the right depth is pure guess work. You might experiment by letting out different amounts of line until you find something that works, then turn the boat around and no longer be at the right depth because a headwind slows your trolling speed.

I avoid the guesswork by using a downrigger with an eight-pound ball. Regardless of wind, boat speed, etc., I know exactly how deep my lure is. In addition, when a kokanee hits I can free the line from the downrigger and play the fish, not the weight. Time after time I've seen a kokanee angler pumping a big rod and reeling so hard I was sure there was a mammoth mackinaw on the line. Then in comes a nine-inch fish preceded by four ounces of lead and a five-blade lake troll. There's a better way, and downriggers are the tool.

When kokanee fishing, I use my ultralight spinning rod, a very small dodger, and no lead. Kokanee are not big, and this light rig puts me in touch with the fish. Without a downrigger, I'd be forced to use heavy sinkers, which means a big rod, which means tackle that overpowers the fish. I once met a kokanee angler who refused to use a downrigger because he felt it was "unsporting." I think it's the other way around.

One key point that many kokanee fishers miss is that the right depth can change depending on several factors, the most important of which is light. Kokanee are very sensitive to sunlight, and while you might think it's pretty dark at 50 or 80 feet, the kokanee don't think so. Too much light turns the fish off. That's why the best fishing is in the morning or evening, or on overcast days. Further, if the wind picks up and puts a riffle on the water, the fish become bolder. The converse is true if the wind dies and the lake goes flat. This means that the depth at which you find biting fish can vary as the weather changes.

On this morning, I tied my usual brass Triple Teaser behind a size 000 brass and silver dodger. A dodger is not necessary (and a five-blade lake trolls is a detriment), but I sometimes use one anyway. The dodge-or-not-to-dodge decision is made scientifically and is based on a single variable: if I feel like putting one on, I do it; otherwise I don't. It's not really necessary to have one because kokanee see quite well. I carry a couple of dodgers because it gives me something to change if the fish aren't biting. The change seldom affects the fishing, but it gives me the illusion of control. A lot of fishing decisions are like that.

After ten minutes of trolling, the rod started to bounce. I shifted the motor to neutral, grabbed the rod from its holder, and stood up. I have yet to find a downrigger release that is sensitive enough to always let go when a fish as small as a kokanee strikes; they usually need a little help. I gave the rod a jerk, the line pulled free, and I brought the kokanee—a fat 12-incher—to the boat. I briefly admired its green back, silvery sides, and forked tail. Then, "crunch," I broke its neck and tossed it in the cooler.

Another fish soon hit, but fell off the hook when it jumped. Then another came in, this one about 13 inches, and it was "crunch" and into the cooler with its siblings.

I hooked two more fish and now had four kokanee in the cooler, three of them over 13 inches. Two more over 13 inches would make a limit. I decided to see how the fishing was elsewhere on the lake, so headed down by the dam, munching a mid-morning snack of a banana and a Snickers bar on the way. The morning was turning warm, and I removed my jacket by 9:00.

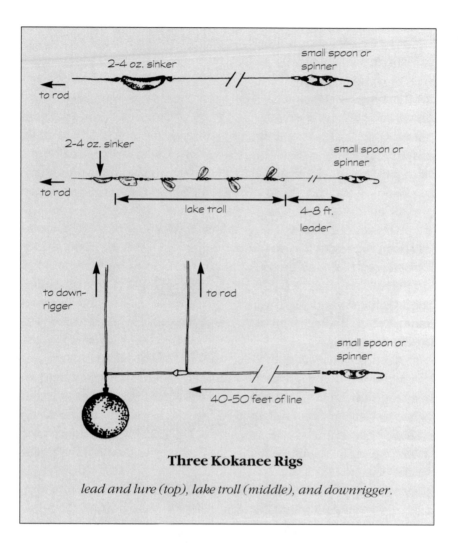

Three Kokanee Rigs

lead and lure (top), lake troll (middle), and downrigger.

Not much was happening around the dam, so I headed back to where I'd started trolling, only I moved closer to shore so I could stay in the shade. A couple more kokanee came in, and I had my limit by 11:00.

After lunch I called Bill Kremers, a friend who lives in Corvallis. "Bill," I said. "I'm having good fishing in Green Peter. What are you doing tomorrow?"

"How good is it?" Bill said.

"I had a size limit before 11:00."

"See you at daybreak."

Bill drove up as I was getting the boat ready to launch. He, too, is a downrigger devotee and has a small portable unit which he clamped to the side of the Klamath. We started in the same area I had fished yesterday, heading west so the sun wouldn't be in our eyes.

Bill uses a long, light-weight bass rod for kokanee. He fills the levelwind reel with a low-stretch braided line. As long as the leader is thin monofilament, the kokanee don't seem to mind the thicker line. The advantage is that it is much easier to tell if you have a strike because the line doesn't stretch. Some monofilament lines have so much stretch that the only way you know you hooked a fish is to raise the downrigger.

We were into fish right away. At first, I'd shift the motor to neutral while whoever hooked a kokanee reeled in, but we had so many hookups that after a while I just let the boat keep trolling. Bill would bring in a fish; "crunch," and it would go into his cooler. Then I'd have one; "crunch," and into my cooler. There was seldom a time when one of us wasn't reeling in a fish or setting up the downrigger for the next pass.

We began releasing fish under 13 inches and only kept the bigger ones. By the time the boat was turned around and we'd made a second pass through the trolling zone, both our coolers held a limit. We were done by 10:00.

Bill's fish were slightly bigger than mine. The primary difference between us was that he used a smaller dodger with a finish that was slightly less flashy. He also used a simple homemade spinner with a few red beads and a silver blade. This confirmed my view that with kokanee, less is more.

After Bill left, I took my mess of kokanee to the fish cleaning station at the campground. By the time I was done, I had two big piles: one was fish ready for the freezer, and the other was fish heads and guts.

Big lifeless eyes looked out on a waterless world. Roe not quite ready for spawning spilled over dark red livers and pale stomachs. Stringy guts and filmy membranes clung to my fingers.

I thought about the bright silver fish that swam in the lake with the funny name. Now they were just two piles: meat and garbage. It was enough for now. The blood lust was sated, and it would be three months before I killed another fish.

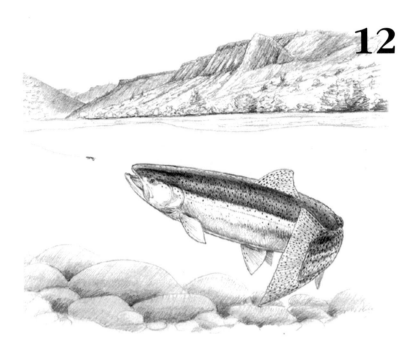

12

Quest for Silver

Late September, Deschutes River below Sherars Falls

I'd known for a couple of years that this would be a good summer for steelhead. Two springs back the weather was wet and cold, which meant young steelhead had an abundance of water in their nursery creeks. Now they were returning as adults in numbers not seen for nearly a decade, so I was sure this was the year Martin would get his steelhead.

Martin James is an Englishman who comes to Oregon every summer for six weeks of fishing. It's a business/pleasure trip because he's a BBC radio broadcaster with a weekly fishing program. Martin has fished all over the world, but his dream was to catch a steelhead on a fly. And not just any steelhead; he wanted an Oregon steelhead, preferably one from the Deschutes River.

I'd met Martin and his wife Kate two years before when we spent an afternoon fishing an Oregon river. A few months later, Barbara and I stayed at their home in Lancashire and spent a week fishing Martin's favorite streams. We became good friends and exchanged letters through the winter. He had ambitious plans for this year's visit to Oregon, but a fly-caught steelhead was the fish he sought most. As we prepared to leave for the Deschutes, we loaded a lot of gear into my truck—raft, rods, food, waders, etc.—but none of it had more substance than Martin's dream.

I had some concerns. On previous visits to Oregon, Martin had hooked three steelhead, none of which stayed stuck more than a few seconds. He had been fishing with some of the state's best steelheaders, people like Bill Baake and Frank Moore. These anglers aren't just good; they're legends. In terms of steelheading talent, I don't come up to their belt buckle. Still, the Deschutes was full of fish, and good odds might conceal my mediocre skill as a guide.

I wasn't settled in my mind as to which part of the Deschutes we should drift. I'd kept track of the fishing for a few weeks before Martin's arrival, but I wasn't sure where we'd find the most fish. Should we put the raft in at Macks Canyon and concentrate on the lower section of the river, or stay farther upstream? I didn't make up my mind until we were bouncing down the access road with our shuttle driver.

"We'll start at Pine Tree and drift to the mouth," I said, sounding more certain than I felt. "That way, if there's a big push of fish coming upriver, we'll run into them." Pine Tree is the second put-in below Sherars Falls. It would give us a forty-mile drift to the Columbia. Surely we'd come across fish somewhere in that route.

"Sounds good," said Martin. "I've never been on the lower river. Maybe I'll be the first Englishman to drift the entire Deschutes."

Our shuttle driver shrugged and said, "Fine with me if I don't have to drive that lower road."

We shoved off a little past noon and hit a couple of runs without success. My plan was to spend the dusk hours fishing at Hole-in-the-Rock, then stay the night at the Beavertail campground. Hole-in-the-Rock is one of my favorite steelhead runs on the river, partly because it's good water, and partly because it's where I hooked my first Deschutes steelhead.

Before we started casting I gave Martin a whistle on a lanyard. "Whistle when you hook a fish. I'll come right away."

He tweeted the whistle for practice, then said, "Come on steelhead. Mike may die."

Martin has a rich East End accent (a dialect most Americans would identify as Cockney or Australian), so it took me a few seconds to sort out this *non sequitur.* I realized he wasn't talking about the potential demise of a friend, but was quoting Clint Eastwood: "Make my day."

I have spent enough time with Martin that I'm getting better with these little translations. I'm still occasionally stumped and beg an explanation of some bit of slang or odd expression, especially with fishing terms such as *trot* (fishing with a moving float), and *leger* (fish using a weight that rests on the bottom), and *buzzers* (midges). I once fished with Martin and a friend of his from Lancashire who has a strong north county accent. He and Martin could talk to each other for fifteen minutes, and I'd have no more clue what they were saying than if they were speaking Mandarin.

On this evening at Hole-in-the-Rock, no fish came along to make either Martin's day or mine. We lingered longer than we should have, stretching the dusk hours in the hope of a fish. By the time we had drifted to Beavertail, it was almost too black to see.

The next morning, we were up before dawn. I wanted to get us to the water around Cedar Island before any other anglers reached it. We packed up quickly, skipped breakfast, and I was parking the raft on the island as it got just light enough to fish.

I started Martin in the middle of the island's west side. It's a good stretch of what some steelheaders call "traveling water," water that steelhead pass through in the morning hours, and is easily covered by a good caster.

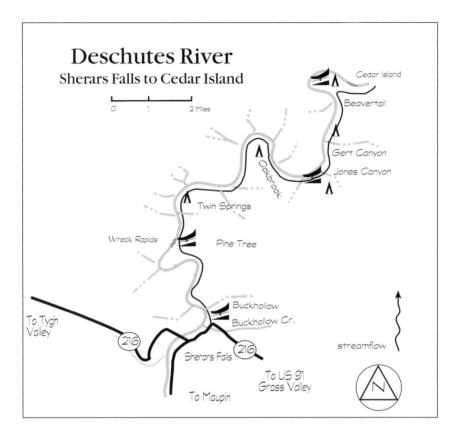

Deschutes River
Sherars Falls to Cedar Island

0 1 2 Miles

Cedar Island
Beavertail
Gert Canyon
Jones Canyon
Oakbrook
Twin Springs
Wreck Rapids
Pine Tree
Buckhollow
Buckhollow Cr.
To Tygh Valley
216
216
Sherars Falls
To US 91 Grass Valley
To Maupin
streamflow
N

I fished the water above Martin where I could keep an eye on him, partly to help if he hooked a fish, and partly for safety. Mornings are a hard time for Martin because his multiple sclerosis bothers him most when he's cold.

The neurological disease hit him over twenty years ago when he was 37. Until then, he'd led an active outdoor life of fishing and shooting. He doesn't talk much about what he did for a living, except to say that it involved "surveillance" and required physical fitness of the highest order. He'd often be at home planning a fishing or hunting trip, then the telephone would ring, and a voice would say something like, "The rooster has crowed." An hour later he'd be on an airplane to some far corner of the world.

Then came a time when he was bothered by sharp "pins and

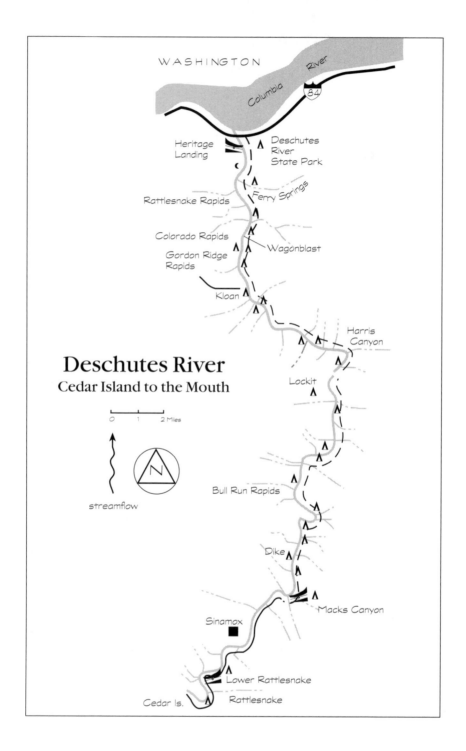

Deschutes River
Cedar Island to the Mouth

0   1   2 Miles

streamflow

WASHINGTON

Columbia River

84

Heritage Landing

Deschutes River State Park

Rattlesnake Rapids

Ferry Springs

Colorado Rapids

Gordon Ridge Rapids

Wagonblast

Kloan

Harris Canyon

Lockit

Bull Run Rapids

Dike

Macks Canyon

Sinamox

Lower Rattlesnake

Cedar Is.

Rattlesnake

needles" in his hands, and sometimes his speech would slur or he'd fall over for no reason. The diagnosis was MS. A brother had the disease, so Martin knew what he faced. He wanted to die.

For several years he was bed-ridden, living in despair and self-pity. Finally a nurse told him to stop feeling sorry for himself and just try. That doesn't work for all MS sufferers, but for Martin it was the advice he needed. With a tremendous exertion of will, he graduated to a wheel chair. And he went fishing, begging someone to push him to a river where he could pursue his beloved chub or cast to marauding pike. Eventually, he got so he could use a walker, then even walk on his own.

His MS is in remission now, but it still bothers him, especially on cold days. He suffers greatly in his hands and feet during the English winters, and even a cool September morning on the Deschutes can make his hands hurt so badly he could weep with frustration and pain. I've been with him when he suddenly lost his voice, and it would be hours before he could talk again. Other times, his legs would stop working. These episodes come without warning, and for this reason I don't like to leave him alone when he wades the river. He is aware of the danger, and always wears an inflatable life jacket.

We cast our way down the west side of Cedar Island without incident, then headed for the east side where we'd left the raft. The easiest passage across the island is to walk the bed of a little creek that flows from west to east. It is a narrow, tree-lined stretch about three-feet wide, and the wading is tricky.

We found the east side still partly shaded, which was good for the fishing. At the top of the island there's a riffle with a seam (a break between fast water and slow) with the slow water on the island side. It's prime steelhead water, and I figured Martin had a 50/50 chance of a hookup, which is pretty good odds for steelheading. I stayed by him because the bottom is rocky, and I didn't want him to take a ducking.

"I had a nice steelhead in this run," I said after he made a few casts. "It was a few years back. Hit right about there." I pointed to some water he would reach in about three more casts. "It took in slow water, then went into the fast current. Ripped line off the reel like I'd hooked a freight train."

"Coor, that sounds lovely." *Coor* is one of those East End expressions that defies translation because it has no meaning other than as a general exclamation of amazement, delight, or shock. It's rather like the Norwegian *uff da*, but means more than the American *oh wow*.

But we passed through that piece of water without a grab. "Pay attention to this next patch," I said. "It's a perfect lie for steelhead."

"How come?"

"See where that creek cuts through the island? The one we walked down? The current from the creek joins the fast current from this riffle. In between there's slow water. Not still, just slow. Steelhead love places like that. I bet there's one in there waiting for you."

We neared the good water, and about the time Martin's fly was going to land in it, a red shape shot out of the creek at great speed. It was a whitewater canoe with a lone paddler; he had crossed the island on the little creek. The canoeist made a sharp turn, looked briefly in our direction, and went his way downriver.

Martin and I stood speechless. In the last hour, we had twice waded that creek. Anglers use it every day, especially in the morning. Visibility is limited, and there is no room to maneuver. If the canoe had gone through while we'd been there, a collision with serious injury would have been unavoidable. It seemed to me that a canoeist with any common sense would have recognized that he could neither maneuver nor stop in that creek, and had no business being there.

Martin finished fishing the run, although there was little point in it since the canoeist had just trashed the water. Any steelhead that had been lying there would have bolted after the canoe swooshed over its head.

We decided to cook breakfast before moving on, and when I opened the cooler I made a terrible discovery. "Martin," I said tentatively, "where's your tea?"

Martin peered into the cooler with deep concern, then checked the contents of his pack. "Coor! I left the jar at home on the kitchen counter."

"I've got some herbal," I said. "Lemon Zinger, Apple Spice . . ."

"It won't do," he said, biting his lip. He squared his shoulders as if he were facing another Blitz. "Well," he said. "I'll just have to make do."

We hit a few more good runs that day, but the hoped-for concentration of fish didn't show itself. By mid-afternoon, we reached Ferry Springs, an outstanding steelhead run a couple of miles above Macks Canyon. Ferry Springs is best fished at dusk with a floating line, but I wanted to try it under sunny conditions and see if a sinking line could dredge up a steelhead. After an hour of casting with a purple woolly bugger, there was a solid pull. I soon had a six-pound hatchery hen on the bank.

"You know," I said as we admired the steelhead's sleek, torpedo-shaped body, "when you catch your steelhead . ."

"If," he interrupted.

"When you catch your steelhead," I repeated, "I'll snap a picture. We'll save the fly and mount it with a print of the fish. You can hang it on the wall of your study."

He smiled grudgingly and nodded. "That would be lovely."

We drifted past Macks Canyon and stopped at Dike, pitching the tent and cooking an early dinner so the evening would be free for fishing. By this time I'd decided evenings would be the best time for Martin because it would be warmer, and his MS would affect him less. I chose Dike because it is on the west bank, so its runs are shaded in the evening.

After cleaning up the dinner dishes, we walked upstream. I started Martin on a good stretch, then moved downstream a couple of hundred feet and began working another piece of water. Ordinarily, I'd have moved farther from another angler, but tonight I wanted to be near Martin because I was sure he'd soon hook a steelhead. He was in the right place at the right time, and doing the right thing.

However, the first fish that showed itself was on my water. I was fifteen minutes into the run when I felt a sharp pluck and the free line zipped out of my hand, but there was no hookup. I knew exactly what had happened: a steelhead had followed the fly and made a pass at it. When this happens, you have found an active fish, one that wants to be a player even though you haven't hooked it. Most of the time, these fish can be brought back to the fly if you cast again.

"Martin," I yelled. "Get down here. There's a fish with your name on it." He was soon in the water near me. I pointed to where the steelhead had nipped my fly. "Start up here," I said, "about six feet higher than I was. Work down to the fish. If it doesn't take, move back up and come down again with a smaller, darker fly." This is standard steelheading doctrine, and I had confidence it would work for Martin.

I left the water and stood on the bank to see if I could spot the flash of a fish. On Martin's second cast, I saw a shape in the river all right, but it was the dark gray of a large raft, not the silver-pink of a steelhead. The rafter passed near Martin, then cut for shore 50 feet downstream from him—right over the water he was fishing.

I uttered—not too quietly—a two-word phrase that simultaneously questioned both the rafter's intelligence and the legitimacy of his birth. I continued in a similar vein as he parked the raft and began unloading. There was no point in fishing the run after the raft ran over it, and Martin left the water with a stricken look on his face.

Once again, I was enraged by the unthinking and callous actions of others. If I'd been alone, it wouldn't have bothered me so much, but I was with a guest from another country, a man whose dream was to catch a steelhead on a fly despite severe physical difficulties, and every time he reached a patch of prime water some bozo would run over it. Among other things, I was embarrassed; my favorite river in all the world seemed to swarm with loutish boaters.

I breathed deeply and tried to stop shaking with anger. The rafter, a trim young man in his late twenties, walked near me. "Did you see that angler out there?" I said.

He looked at the water. "Yes. I thought I gave him enough room."

I shook my head. "He was casting to the water you passed over."

"I wanted to camp here." He pointed to a campsite in the trees.

I glanced into his raft; there were no rods or fishing gear. I shrugged. "How would you know," I said. "You're not an angler."

He dropped his head and stared at the ground by his left sandal. "Uh . . . right," he said. "Right."

There were no fish that night, nor the next morning. After breakfast I made a decision: we'd drift fifteen miles to Wagonblast, a section of river five miles from the mouth. It's one of the best steelhead runs on the river. We'd stay there two nights and catch fish until our arms fell off.

I had one major-league concern about this strategy. Martin unknowingly brought it up after we were underway. "You know that bloke who ran over my fish last night?" he said. "His father wandered through camp while you were loading the raft. He said his son was one of the top guides on the river and a brilliant caster."

"You mean, he really was a fisherman, and he ran through your water anyway?"

"Sounds like it."

There is a problem with this part of the river: competition. It does strange things to people. The lower 24 miles of the Deschutes—especially the lower eight miles—has the best steelheading on the river. Fish bound for other streams duck into the Deschutes for a shot of cooler water, so there are more fish here than anywhere else. And more anglers.

Not all of them are amateurs, either. Many guides work this water, and most of them use jet boats. Those boats are expensive, and to make the payments the guides have to take a lot of clients and keep them happy. The result is that competition for the best water is fierce, and people have come to blows over it, even threat-

Deschutes River Etiquette

Manners are contagious. Perpetuate good ones.

If someone is fishing near where you want to fish, ask if they mind if you fish above or below them.

If someone is fly fishing a run for steelhead, they are probably working their way downstream a step at a time. Don't wade into the river below them, or upstream near them. In general, stay at least 150 yards away.

If you are in a boat or raft, give bank anglers a wide berth. Stay at least 30 feet from where they are casting to, and pass by quietly, without splashing or making other noises that will be transmitted throughout the water.

Don't pull your boat or raft into a backeddy until you are sure no one is fishing it. Leave a camp or rest area looking better than you found it.

Recognize that sun, wind, and exercise are "stressors" that can make you act and feel intoxicated with less alcohol than usual.

ened each other with firearms. Guides guard their favorite runs with jealous zeal, and many anglers, professional and otherwise, abandon politeness in the name of more and bigger fish.

Even normally pleasant people can be caught up in the "every angler for himself" attitude. No doubt that's what happened last night. That rafter is probably a decent guy, but the mentality of the lower river got the better of him. I know it's trapped me; there were times I didn't like the angler I became down here.

In an effort to ease the competition for good fishing water (government bureaucrats call it "user conflicts"), rules have been established to limit powerboat traffic on the lower river. During the prime season, four days—Thursday through Sunday—out of every fourteen are reserved exclusively for drift craft. It's a great idea, and was enacted despite heavy opposition.

Today was Wednesday, and I had no idea whether we were entering a period with or without jet boats. As we neared Wagonblast, several of them roared up and down the river. "Bloody awful things," Martin muttered. "Why do you allow them at all?"

"Get used to it," I said. "We may be living with them for the next two days."

One boat thundered by, headed downriver with a load of clients. A quarter of an hour later it passed us again, headed upstream to an elaborate camp. After we drifted another mile, we saw it for the last time, going downstream with all the camp gear.

"Yes! Yes!" I exulted. "They're leaving! We own the river!"

And we did. As before, I picked a campsite on the west side. No one else was camped there, so one mile of prime bankwater was ours. At last, Martin could catch his steelhead.

The next morning, I was up before Martin. I thought about waking him, but it had been a cool night and he looked tired. I decided to let him sleep.

I headed downstream to cast over a couple of nice-looking runs. The Wagonblast area is about a mile long, and all of it is outstanding fishing from either bank. The river has sculpted many ledges, channels, and drops, and boulders are strewn everywhere. It is perfect "holding water" for resting steelhead.

I started through a short, ledgy run about 200 feet downstream from camp. There were no grabs, so I moved to another run just below it. It had a nice, slow feel, but the river's surface showed enough bumps and grinds to reveal an uneven bottom structure. Behind a boulder, at about the limit of my casting, there was a perfect piece of water. I reached for it, and a fish soon had my fly in its mouth.

Steelhead grab in different ways. Sometimes, it's a slam that rips your arm off, sometimes a slow tightening that builds and builds, and sometimes, like this fish, it's a quick jerk, then a hard pull—a one-two punch that releases energy like a thunderbolt. After what can be hours of tedious casting, the sudden take of a strong fish is such a rush that I can never remember what was happening just before. I've heard that traumas are like that.

When steelheading, the take is what you wait for. You might need 700 or even a thousand casts to hook just one fish, but when that fish comes, the release of tension and rush of adrenaline makes it seem worthwhile. I've landed enough steelhead that I no longer care whether I beach another one or not. Ninety percent of the fun is in the first five minutes, 80% in the first 30 seconds. As one angling friend put it, "You live for the grab."

This fish stayed on until I had it at the bank. I yelled for Martin, and he arrived just as I was releasing it. And he had some news for me.

"I hooked a fish," he said. "About twelve pounds. I saw it jump a couple of times."

I didn't even know he was awake. "Did you land it?" I asked expectantly.

"It came off after about ten minutes." He sighed. "I feel gutted. My hands are still shaking." He sat on a rock and held his arm out like he was playing a fish. A smile came across his face as he relived it.

"I thought you were still asleep," I said.

"No, young man, I've been fishing." He fingered the lanyard around his neck. "I whistled a couple of times."

I was puzzled, then realized the wind blew upstream, carrying the sound away from me. "Didn't hear a thing," I said. "I'm sorry I wasn't there to help."

"It's all right," Martin said, enthusiasm returning to his voice. "We'll just have to find another, won't we."

I hoped so. It was one thing for me to be ambivalent about landing a steelhead I'd hooked, but it was different for Martin because he'd never had the pleasure of bringing one to the bank. Martin's loss diminished the joy my own fish had brought.

That evening I was by his side when he went through a good-looking run. Suddenly his rod bent and there was a boil in the river. But the fish came off as quickly as it had struck. "You know," I said, "I think you may be striking at the fish. When you're after steelhead with a fly rod, you're better off to just swing the rod to the bank when you feel a take. The fish will hook itself."

The next morning there was a sheen of frost on the ground. The nights had been growing cooler, and last night Martin had slept in most of the clothes he'd brought. The cold affected his hands, and he kept flexing his fingers to alleviate the pain.

Another steelhead hit his fly, but it came off right away, as had the previous night's fish. He sat on the bank while I worked a short, bouldery run. I had a take, but the steelhead ran upstream, and I never was able to tighten on it. The barbless hook fell out.

We moved down to another run, just below where I'd caught my fish the day before. It was beautiful water, and I started Martin through it and helped him wade. Even so, the bottom soon grew too rocky for him, and he turned the run over to me.

I waded to the limits of my neoprenes to reach a boulder I could climb onto. From there, I could just reach a wonderful patch of water, and just where I thought it should happen, my line straitened, zipped across the water, then lifted and bowed the rod. This fish stayed on, and Martin took pictures of it before I released it.

We broke camp and left shortly after that. Both of us would have loved to stay another day, maybe more, but the food was almost gone, and Martin had someplace he had to be that afternoon.

As we drifted the river below Rattlesnake Rapids, we passed a great blue heron standing on a rock. "Looking for a little something for his afternoon tea," Martin said.

"You'll be able to get some tea for yourself now," I said.

"Yes, I'm looking forward to that. A burger at the Oasis and a cup of tea. Coor! That will be nice." He put his feet up and basked in the warming day. "It's been a wonderful trip," he said. "I enjoyed every minute of it."

And it had been a good trip. The weather was grand, the company delightful, and I'd hooked four steelhead and landed three. But Martin went fishless.

He put a good face on it. Martin loves the Deschutes as much as anyone I know, taking pleasure in its scenery and wildlife, growing excited at every heron and kingfisher, osprey and otter. But what he wanted—what both of us wanted—more than anything else had not happened. His enthusiasm and energy would carry him through, but disappointment was mingled with the pain and fatigue his illness brought him. It lined his face, tinged his voice, spoke in the sag of his shoulders.

The Deschutes has many virtues, but compassion is not one of them.

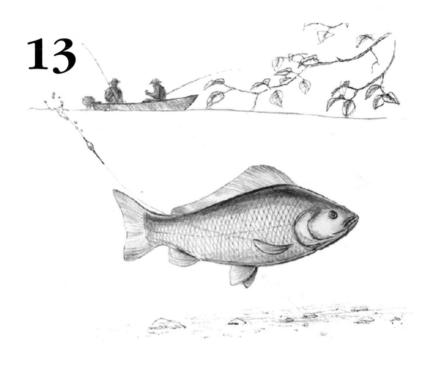

Trash

September, Willamette River near West Linn

L ook at that fish!" Martin said. "Not a scale out of place, and what beautiful colors." He held the fish while I took a picture. "It's in fine shape, perfect condition," he went on. "You Oregonians are lucky to have fish like this so close to home. A lot of Brits would give their eye teeth to have what you have." He lowered the fish and returned it to the river. I've rarely seen anyone handle a fish with as much gentleness and respect. "Coor!" he said. "Now that's what I call having your string pulled! Let's get another one."

Was this a salmon? Or maybe a trophy rainbow trout? Perhaps

Martin's long awaited and much sought steelhead? It was none of these cherished prizes. It was a carp.

Trash fish. The phrase summarizes loathing and deep-felt antipathy. Despicable; worse than useless; usurpers of valuable habitat that rightfully belongs to more respectable fish; dwellers in polluted waters, who thrive near sewage plants and feed on the disgusting waste of civilization; undesirable aliens crowding out native species.

To most Oregon anglers, carp are the ultimate piscatorial trash. But carp are the number one sport fish in Europe. And maybe, someday, in America.

English anglers rhapsodize about their carp. They speak of them in reverent terms, ascribe superior intelligence to them, spend vast sums for the privilege of catching one, invent new ways to trick them. And, like Martin, they are ardent catch-and-releasers of a fish that most Americans view as water-dwelling vermin, golden rats prowling garbage-dump rivers—trash fish.

British anglers fish for anything that swims. There are people who spend tens of thousands of dollars for a 25-foot single-piece graphite rod they will use to catch fish no more than three inches long. Others will spend the equivalent of $700 for one-week's access to a muddy five-acre pond in an industrial area, where they will live in a tent, eat canned beans, and devote their entire vacation to simultaneously watching three expensive rods for some sign of a nibbling carp.

In England, any fish without an adipose fin is, by definition, a coarse fish. This includes carp, pike, perch, chub, rudd, barbel, tench, and a host of other species, most of which have never seen America. Until the middle 1960s, the majority of British fishers were coarse anglers. Then stillwater fly fishing grew in popularity, and now fly and coarse anglers are roughly equal in number. But traditional attitudes die hard. While class privilege has lessened some, English fish and fishing still has class undertones: the aristocrats pur-

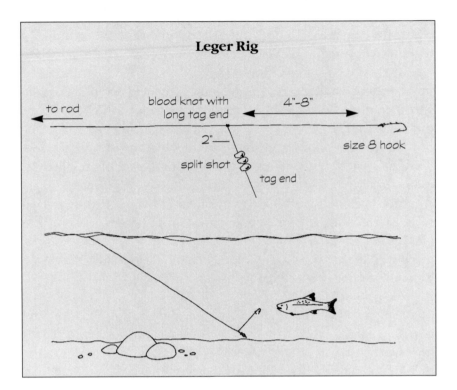

Leger Rig

to rod

blood knot with
long tag end

4"-8"

2"—

split shot

tag end

size 8 hook

sue Atlantic salmon; the upper-middle class seek trout in rivers; and the rest are allowed to catch coarse fish and trout in reservoirs. Few salmon anglers will lower themselves to catch a perch or a carp.

I steered the boat while Martin stood in the bow and scanned the Willamette for signs of carp. Below a rocky point, he motioned for me to slow the boat. "Look at that!" he said, pointing to a line of bubbles that stretched for 100 feet. "I've never seen anything like it. I'll bet there's some 20 pounders in that lot."

"What makes all the bubbles?" I asked.

"Carp root around on the bottom, stirring up the muck and eating midge larvae. And anything else they can find." He looked at the bubbles some more and assessed the current. "How deep is it?"

I checked the locator. "Twenty-three feet."

"Move upstream a bit," he said. "By the time those bubbles reach the surface, they've drifted downstream. The fish are up there." He waved his hand forward.

I switched to the electric motor and we quietly crept into place and anchored. "So, Professor James," I said. "what's the best way to catch these guys?"

"It's too deep for float fishing, so we'll leger crust."

I translated in my mind: *leger*=fish with the weight on the bottom; *crust*=bread.

Martin rigged up with a sinker heavy enough to stay in one place in the gentle current. It was followed by a leader and a #8 barbless hook. He pulled some bread slices from a bag and tore off a piece with the crust on it. He folded the bread carefully so the crust was on the outside and threaded it onto the hook.

"Why bread?" I asked.

"It floats. It will raise off the bottom, and cruising carp will find it by smell. If the bread comes off, it will float and we'll see it. That's how we'll know it's time to re-bait."

We sat in the boat watching our lines for signs of fish. After half an hour, Martin said quietly, "There's one." He waited until the time was right (a moment no angler can define) and set the hook.

His twelve-foot custom-built carp rod hooped into a semi-circle and line ripped from the reel. After a five-minute fight the fish was at the boat. "About eight pounds," Martin said, slightly disappointed. "I was hoping for a double."

Again, I translated in my mind: *double*=double-digit weight; a fish of ten pounds or more. Martin admired the carp, then carefully released it. He rigged up another bread crust and cast it. "Nothing like getting your stick bent," he said.

Although he was born in 1937, Martin James says his life started in 1941—when he caught his first fish during a bomber raid. Martin's home county of Kent was on the front lines of the Battle of Britain, and he grew up with the scream of air raid sirens, the crumph of German bombs, and the roar of Hurricanes and Spitfires.

On his first fishing trip, his Uncle Len took him to a clay pit near the Higham canal. Martin was landing his fifth rudd when a

Hurricane fighter plane raced across the tree tops toward a bomber group. Soon a German plane was falling to earth, and a parachute appeared. "They've got a Jerry!" Martin's Uncle Len said, "We must get the Home Guard."

"You go," said Martin. "I want another fish."

Fishing gave meaning and shape to Martin's life, especially during the war. Before his first fishing trip, his parents were killed by the Japanese in the Far East. He was raised and adopted by his nanny. Uncle Len died in North Africa a few weeks after he took Martin fishing, and a German land mine, dropped to earth by parachute, killed 11 of his young schoolmates. Near the end of the war, a V-1 rocket leveled his home.

Martin grew up fishing clay pits, ponds, canals, saltwater—any place he could put a line. When he became expert with rod and reel, he sought carp, which at that time British anglers considered to be an uncatchable fish. "Carp," Martin has explained to me, "are the most intelligent freshwater fish in the world. Biologists in England, Israel, and Japan all agree: no fish is smarter than a carp."

Biologists in these three countries study carp for reasons as diverse as their cultures. The English revere carp as a sportfish, and carp fishing and tackle are big business. The Israelis raise carp for gefilte fish, a Jewish delicacy. The Japanese value them for ornamental ponds; they say carp will recognize their master's footsteps and gather near him when he approaches.

The reasons fish biologists think carp are so smart is their ability to learn. That's why they're hard to catch in England: after a few catch-and-release sessions they learn to detect the difference between a bait with a hook in it and an identical but harmless bait.

To counter this, hard-core carp anglers go to extremes of ingenuity. They will take a kernel of corn and remove the meat from the membrane, replacing it with styrofoam. This counteracts the minuscule (but detectable by carp) weight of the hook. They make fancy terminal rigs where the hook is not even in the bait. They even use water-soluble string to sink a ring of "boilies" (like doughballs) near a hooked boily. A carp picks up the loose boilies and feels no resistance, then sucks in the one with the hook in it. And these are just a few of the tricks.

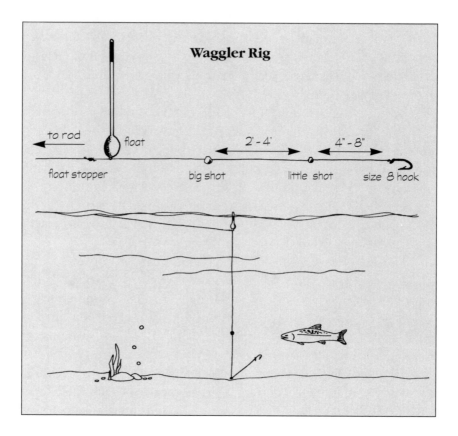

Waggler Rig

to rod

float

float stopper

2' - 4'

big shot

4" - 8"

little shot

size 8 hook

Very few spring creek, upstream dry-fly purists devote this much time, thought, and invention to the pursuit of fish.

While English carp have Ph.D.s in angler detection, Oregon carp are as innocent as daisies, which is why Martin likes to fish for them. It's like a Northwest angler going to a country that teems with blissfully ignorant steelhead that no one fishes for because the local anglers prefer to catch frogs ("we go for 'em at night when they're sittin' on the lily pads. Now that's *real* sport.").

The bubbles stopped and no more fish came to Martin's or my bread crust. We up-anchored and motored about, poking into back bays and eddies and looking for more carp signs. At one spot we saw a huge splash. "There's one!" Martin said. "Pull into here."

"Why do they jump?"

"I don't know, but they all do it. They're very surface-oriented."

"I've seen them at dawn when I've been salmon fishing," I said. "Big heads poking up like huge, scaley trout sipping midges."

"It could have been that. They like midges, and feed on the surface when the light is low."

"Can you catch them on a fly?"

"I've done it," Martin said. He explained how to make a carp fly: "Put a hook in your vise, then dab some superglue on the shank. Stick a dog biscuit on it and you have a carp fly."

"A dog biscuit?" I asked.

"I think you call them kibbles."

I contemplated a future fly tying exhibition where I, a carp expert, would explain to attentive anglers the proper method of tying carp flies: "Select a good kibble, not too old or stale. And use Purina instead of Friskies; they're very selective about that . . ."

I shook my head and returned to the present. "Are we going to leger crust here?" I asked

"No. Too shallow. We'll use the waggler method."

The waggler method is fishing bait—in this case, kernels of corn—from a float. Americans might call this bobber fishing, but the English float is as far from the typical American red-and-white plastic bobber as a Rolls Royce is from a tricycle. English floats are finely crafted from balsa or other light-weight woods. They are carefully counterbalanced so the slightest touch makes them move, and they are designed so the line between the rod and the float is underwater. This latter innovation reduces wind drift.

We rigged up two rods and cast out. After a bit, Martin's float began to rise. "Wouldn't it sink if a fish had taken it?" I asked.

"Sometimes they raise up. If Mr. Carp hoovers up the bait, the shot on the bottom comes up and the float will rise, not sink."

He set the hook and brought another carp to the boat. "Oooh, nice mirror carp," he said, pointing out the few large scales on the carp. "The other one I caught is what we call the common carp. They have scales all over. At home, we have a scaleless species called the leather carp, but you don't have them here."

He gently released the carp and re-cast. Soon it was my float's turn to bob. I yanked hard on my rod and felt nothing.

"Too soon," Martin said. "Wait longer next time. Of course, your fish bite quickly compared to ours. An English carp might mess about with the bait for an hour."

I took a deep breath and cast again. Soon, my float was bobbing up and down. This time I waited.

"Floats," said Martin, quoting an English maxim, "are pleasing in their appearance, and even more pleasing in their disappearance."

Mine disappeared, I struck, and this time met solid resistance. Line peeled off the spinning reel, then came grudgingly back. Martin netted the fish and handed it to me.

"You hold it," he said, "while I snap a photo. Rock it back and forth first. That makes the dorsal fin stand up."

I rocked the fish, and Martin tripped the shutter. "Do you think," I said, "that when you print that photo, you could put black tape over my eyes so no one will know it's me?"

It was not my first carp. When I was a boy, I would trundle my rod and gear down to Seattle's Lake Washington Ship Canal and fish for them with canned corn. There were some big ones down there, and I often had success. I'd take each one home, and my mother would bury it under a rhododendron. The rhodies thrived on them.

Once, while walking home with three big carp, I passed a neighbor's house where a team of Japanese gardeners were manicuring the lawn. One old guy saw my carp and got very excited. He ran up to me shouting, "Koi, koi!"

If I'd had any sense, I'd have given him the fish. If I'd been clever, I'd have traded them for a lawn mowing job, which would release me for more fishing time. Being 15 years old, however, I didn't know what to do or say and kept walking. The shrubs appreciated the fish, though.

Those jaunts to the ship canal were cultural expeditions as well as fishing trips. It was the first place I met black people (at that time they weren't allowed to buy homes in my neighborhood), Hungarian immigrants, and other ethnic people. On that urban water, fishing was a sport where class and race faded in importance.

But I grew up and pursued more "respectable" fish, such as trout, in more classic places, such as mountain lakes. Carp became quarry for children and ethnic minorities, and I was neither. Trout were the fish for adult WASPs like me, and a fly rod was a gentleman's tool.

In time, I became a fly-fishing prig: anyone who didn't fish with the long rod was a lesser being and unworthy of notice. Fortunately, I got over it (some fly fishers never do) and came to value other fishing methods and other fish. Now I feel as if I've entered a new phase, an egalitarian state akin to the best ideals of the French Revolution, but without the nasty side-effects.

Carp fishing with Martin, however, provided the severest test of my piscatorial *liberté, egalité, fraternité*. I could understand the attraction of the fish. They are wary and cautious, like brown trout; hard fighters, like chinook; they could even be taken on a fly like brook trout. So what was this uneasy feeling in the pit of my stomach?

I went through the arguments against carp. First, you can't eat them. Well, that argument didn't hold water; I release most of my catch anyway.

Second, they're ugly. But I'd seen Martin treat carp with grace and care, and he thought they were beautiful. I remembered the golden iridescence of the scales, and I had to admit it was a pretty sight when considered with an open mind. The mouth is not lovely, but then neither is a bonefish's, and people go into ecstasies about bonefish. And when brown trout were first introduced to America, anglers regarded them as ugly. They still don't win any beauty contest when compared to brook trout and rainbows, but I've never heard someone who just landed a five-pound brown talk about how repulsive it looked.

The third argument against carp is that they inhabit polluted water. It is true that carp have a high tolerance for water conditions. They are a goldfish, so they can live in anything from pure water to murky, high-temperature ponds. They are survivors. Should that be counted against them? And in the Willamette River, where Martin and I fished for carp, they rub fins with salmon, smallmouth bass, walleye, and sturgeon.

Fourth and last, it can be said that carp are not a native species and therefore have no right to be here. Yet, I love to fish for brook trout, and they're not natives of the Northwest. Further, carp are as alien to American waters as that other European native, the brown trout.

None of the arguments against carp survived scrutiny. If I was going to reject carp as a viable Oregon sportfish, I'd have to toss out a few other species for the sake of consistency.

As I disposed of my reservations about carp, I began broaching the subject to hot-shot fly anglers just to get a rise out of them. Usually, I got an uneasy is-this-guy-for-real politeness. Sometimes it was more like humor-him, he-might-be-violent. A few people, however, have expressed interest is going carp fishing with me, and usually they are the most experienced and knowledgeable anglers. And I'm talking about several guys, not just one or two kinky weirdos.

Why are they interested? I think it's because they've spent so much time on the water that they have come to value everything that swims. They no longer have to prove themselves to others, and feel free to explore all things fishy.

Not every angler has this attitude. I've fished on the Deschutes with people who despised whitefish, which are as native as the resident redside trout. One angler I know took an inexperienced friend to the lower Deschutes and left him on his own for a while. When he returned, the neophyte proudly displayed his catch, a big whitefish. "Do you think it will taste good?" he asked. My acquaintance grabbed the fish and threw it up the bank. "That's a whitefish," he said with disgust. Then in the crudest slang, he mentioned two non-white minorities. "No one eats whitefish but *them*," he said.

His response revealed a dark side of human nature that wants to class everybody as us and them, and do it without the bother of finding out what the other person is really made of. Skin color is one quick way to do this. Religion is another, and fishing technique and the kind of fish you pursue can be just another excuse for bigotry. "You are what you catch," is the attitude. "Coarse fish are for coarse people."

A lot of fly fishers think they've reached the acme of angling because they use a long rod and are into catch-and-release. Besides, there is an English aristocratic tradition behind the sport, so it has an air of gentility.

However, the first catch-and-release anglers in Britain were the lowly coarse fishermen. More than 150 years ago they recognized that they'd soon have no sport if they killed their catch, no matter how much their "betters" despised it. So they released their fish.

In the 1930s, Lee Wulff told Americans that trout were too valuable to be caught only once, and he gave birth to a movement that has improved fishing wherever it is practiced in the U.S. But the English commoner had been preaching that gospel, in a lower-class accent, for nearly a century before Wulff articulated it.

In the meantime, the British aristocracy killed every wild trout and salmon they got their hands on. And they're still doing it. In an age when wild Atlantic salmon would make the endangered species list (if the U.K. had such a thing), most upper-class British sportsmen bonk every salmon they land with a wooden club called a "priest," as if a religious connotation would put a blessing on the slaughter. While the thoughtless exploitation of unearned resources has a long tradition among the aristocracy, it's an attitude that should make a one-way trip to Madame La Guillotine.

Given a choice between the coarse fisherman in his cloth cap and funny dialect, and the aristocrat with his tweeds and bland intonations, I'd rather adopt the angling traditions of the former.

There are no trash fish, just trash attitudes. There is only one way to measure a person's worth as an angler, and it's not by the species fished for, how the bait, lure, or fly is put in front of the fish, or even the size or number of the catch. The only yardstick is the angler's attitude toward the quarry: does he value fish enough to learn all he can about them, and does he take care of them? Nothing else counts.

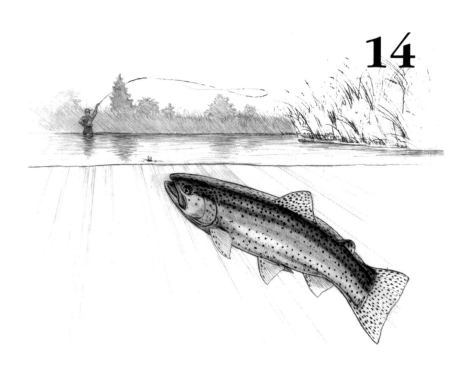

Southern Shadows

Early October, Lower Williamson River near Chiloquin

It was the kind of weather that grabs your nose with one cold hand and slaps your cheeks with the other. Fog lay on the river so thick I could barely see the water from the boat, and the mist had frozen onto bankside willows and sedges, giving them thick white coats. I wouldn't have minded a thicker coat myself. And thicker socks; my toes felt like popsicles—the purple kind.

Less than two weeks ago, when Martin and I started our drift down the Deschutes, my sweat-soaked T-shirt was sticking to my back. Now I was wearing all the clothes in my duffel bag. How did it get so cold so fast? Last night the thermometer hit the teens—the low teens—before dawn, and I'd spent a chilly night in the back of the truck because I'd brought my summer-weight sleeping bag. After breakfast, the shock of the cold toothbrush sent my teeth into convulsions.

On this arctic morning in early October, I launched the boat at Chiloquin, sliding it down a steep, dirt ramp near the airstrip. It was a launch that required finesse: stop too soon and the boat wouldn't reach the water; stop too late and I'd be calling a tow truck. I was lucky today. The boat slid into the river, and the truck didn't.

I rowed through the fog and anchored in a place that seemed as good as any, but I couldn't tell for sure. With frozen fingers, I tied an olive Woolly Bugger onto a twelve-foot leader fastened to a sinking line, and cast to where I heard (maybe) a rise. No luck there. As the fog thinned, I could see more ledges and rocks, and I probed them with the Woolly Bugger. After half an hour, I had a hard pull without a hookup. I persisted in casting, hoping for another grab. I figured the excitement of hooking a big trout would be the only thing that could stir my blood enough to keep my toes from falling off.

The Williamson River flows into Upper Klamath Lake north of the town of Klamath Falls. In its lower reaches, the river is slow, almost lake-like in places, but has surprising drops and ledges. Trout can be lurking behind, in front of, or alongside any of these structures. Some of those trout weigh over ten pounds.

The Williamson is rich enough to nourish good-sized fish on its own, but the really big ones come up from the lake, seeking relief from July's heat. The lake was my reason for coming here. In January, fishing guide Denny Rickards invited me to pursue its big rainbows. "Last year," he'd said, "I caught and released more than 800 rainbows over four pounds. Many of them pushed eight pounds or more; some were around 15 pounds."

This sort of talk always gets my attention, and we'd kept in touch throughout the season, trying to find a mutually convenient time to fish. May was a possibility but proved too cold to turn the fish on, so we'd postponed until June, a month that proved no bet-

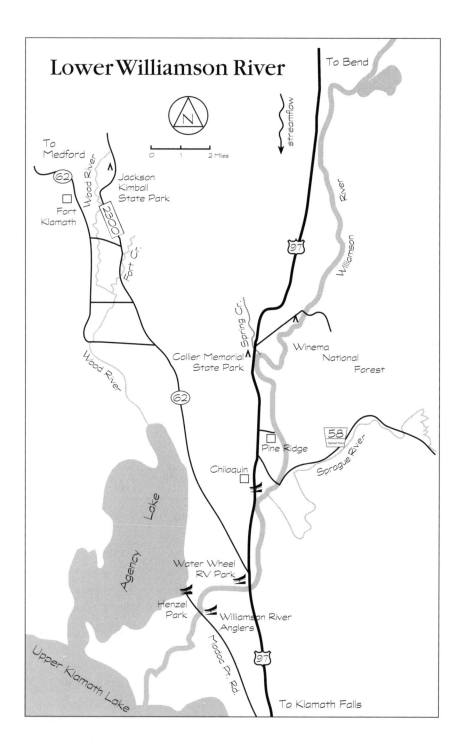

Lower Williamson River

To Bend

streamflow

To Medford

Jackson Kimball State Park

Wood River

62

2300

Fort Klamath

Fort Cr.

Williamson River

97

Spring Cr.

Collier Memorial State Park

Winema National Forest

Wood River

62

58
National Forest

Pine Ridge

Sprague River

Chiloquin

Lake

Agency

Water Wheel RV Park

Henzel Park

Williamson River Anglers

Upper Klamath Lake

Modoc Pt. Rd.

97

To Klamath Falls

N

0   1   2 Miles

ter than its predecessor. July passed without a trip to Oregon's southland, and when Denny had good fishing in August, I was elsewhere. September came and was mostly gone before we settled on a date, and the first week of October I was trailering my driftboat down US 97 to Klamath County.

In Oregon, summer is slow to come and often quick to leave, so I knew this might be my last chance at lake fishing for half a year. If it didn't warm up, I wouldn't even have a last shot at Crane Prairie.

My plan was to fish the local rivers for two days before meeting Denny. I stopped first at Williamson River Anglers, a fly shop just south of Chiloquin. I asked the shop owner how the fishing had been in the Williamson.

"Worst in nine years," she said.

I hate conversations that begin like this.

"Last year it was phenomenal," she said. "Did you come then?"

"No."

"This year the lake is the fullest its been in 90 years, and it's stayed cool, so the fish haven't come into the rivers."

"Oh."

She eyed my driftboat which was parked outside the shop. "Do you want a shuttle?" she said.

"Are there . . . you know . . . a *few* rainbows around?"

A customer who was looking at flies lifted his head. "I've fished for three days," he said, "and I didn't see any." He thought a moment, then said, "I might have seen one. Day before yesterday. Couldn't be sure, though. It was great last year."

"Do you want a shuttle tomorrow morning?" the shop owner queried again.

I shrugged. "Might as well."

So it came to pass that on a frigid morning I skidded the boat down the rutted dirt ramp and searched the river for trout. I knew the Williamson is not an easy river to fish. First, it runs clear, so the fish see every mistake you make. Next, its drops and ledges are unpredictable. They hold fish, but if you don't know the river's structure like the back of your rod hand, you can easily miss the best places. And last, many of the trout have moved up from the lake, and the narrow confines of a river make them extra wary.

In past seasons I'd made two trips to the Williamson, with dubious results both times. On the first visit, Bob Jones and I spent two days fishing with a singularly uninspired guide who should have retired a couple of years before we arrived. We caught a few fish around 12 inches and a sunburn. The next year I came back and spent an afternoon and evening getting thoroughly skunked, and retreated to the Deschutes the next day. I figured today couldn't be worse than my other two trips.

This part of the Williamson is not what you'd call *wilderness.* It's pretty enough, with summer-tanned grasses and ponderosa pines lining the bank, but its proximity to US 97 means you're never far from the rumble of trucks and cars. At first, I heard them through the early morning mist, then shape was added to sound as the day warmed and the fog lifted.

The clearing air also revealed a large fish rising near a shrub on the left bank. It only made one rise every ten minutes or so, but I had a glimpse of it. It looked to be around four pounds and had the pastel tints of a brown trout. I still harbored hopes of a big brown; none had bowed my rod this year. After each rise I'd drift a fly near this trout, get no take, then cast elsewhere until the next rise.

When fishing is slow and I'm on an unfamiliar river, I develop more theories than a philosophy professor (usually with equal practicality in the real world). In this case, I theorized that the cold weather would slow the fish down, and they would be found in slow water near the bottom. I clipped off the Woolly Bugger, changed reel spools to a Type III sinker, and dredged the river with a big brown Matuka. If there were any fish around, they found the Matuka no more attractive than the Woolly Bugger.

By noon it had warmed into the low forties—a veritable heat wave—and I could actually feel my toes. I up-anchored and drifted through a very rocky and shallow rapids, the kind of water rafters call "technical." After careful maneuvering that avoided every single rock, I gave myself 10 points for style and anchored near some good-looking water. Self-congratulation ended quickly, however, when I realized I'd just parked the boat in the best holding water around. That's the problem with the Williamson: unless you know the river, you either screw up the good spots or pass them by.

Just downstream, however, I saw small rises in a foam line below a riffle. I couldn't see what they were rising to, but I could see the trout clearly, all six or seven inches of them.

I soon picked up a few of these little guys and moved on. I felt better because I'd had my string pulled, but I also felt worse. I had the uneasy feeling that being satisfied with small fish indicated a serious character deficiency, as if I'd gone hunting for tigers but was just as happy to pop a couple of squirrels.

By 2:15 I'd fished for six and half hours and covered 500 yards of river. Coming around a bend, I saw more risers and picked up more seven inchers. Some rises appeared on the other side of the boat, but when I cast to them, they stopped. I waited two minutes, then cast again. The fly disappeared in a fishy swirl, the rod bowed, line came off the reel, and in the river a respectable 14-inch trout did a cartwheel. It chased away all my guilty feelings about casting to small fish.

For the rest of the afternoon, I drifted the river and looked for rises. I picked up a few more dinks and another 14-incher. Near dusk, I anchored alongside a promising riffle. When I stood up to survey the water I realized that—once again—I'd parked the boat too close to the best water.

Then I saw the shadow dropping slowly away from me, moving purposely to midriver, then sinking out of vision. My mental scale estimated the fish's size: eight pounds easy; ten probably; more, maybe. I became aware that I was slack-jawed and staring. I waited a few moments before casting to where the huge trout disappeared. I fished until the end of daylight but hooked nothing.

Upper Williamson River at Yamsi Ranch

About 60 miles upstream from where I'd fished the previous day, springs bubble up from the earth and give birth to the Williamson River. Most of those springs are on Yamsi Ranch, a 5,000 acre spread on a high plateau in the Basin and Range country east of Klamath Falls.

In less than a quarter mile, the springs merge their flows to produce a fifty-foot wide spring creek. It meanders through open, grassy meadows, looking like those rivers they're always showing in magazines, but that you rarely encounter in real life. Eventually it comes to the soggy depression of Klamath Marsh.

The river loses its way when it reaches the marsh, then finds it again on the other side. Below Klamath Marsh, the Williamson's fish are mostly rainbows and a few brown trout out of Klamath Lake. Above the marsh, the fish are rainbows and brook trout. The marsh keeps fish from the two parts of the river from mingling and forms the dividing point between the upper and lower Williamson.

Yamsi is owned by Dayton and Gerda Hyde. It is an example of how rural land owners can preserve wild fish while earning extra cash. In addition to the 500 head of cattle that munch Yamsi's grass, up to ten guests at a time munch Gerda's excellent food and stay in antique-filled rooms in the old stone ranch house. All that, and they get to fish. Or, as Gerda Hyde says, "We charge $200 a day for the fishing; the meals and lodging are free."

And what outstanding fishing it is. The upper Williamson twists and turns across five miles of Yamsi's gorgeous meadows. Every bend holds plump trout, either rainbows or brookies. The upper river has not been stocked for years, so the rainbows are both wild and native, and the brookies are wild. Both grow big. Brook trout are typically three or four pounds, rainbows a pound more. The biggest fish taken from the ranch property was a 31-inch 'bow that probably weighed nine or ten pounds.

After my cold float on the lower Williamson, I decided to spend a day investigating the region's private fisheries. I was too broke to actually pay for the fishing at Yamsi, but Dayton Hyde's son John and his son-in-law Scott graciously showed me what the ranch had to offer.

We walked across the open ground, slowing as we approached the river. "There's some," John said. "See them?"

I shifted to polarized sunglasses and let my eyes adjust to the river. Several large shadows milled lazily in the current. "Whoa!" I said, totally impressed. "Nice fish!"

John shrugged. "Average."

In midriver a brook trout rose and took a drifting bug from the surface. "Is it mostly dry fly fishing?" I asked.

"A mix of dries and nymphs," John said. "We use a variety of patterns. They can be pretty selective." He grinned. "I think we've educated them a bit."

"It's catch-and-release?"

John nodded, "Barbless flies only and release all fish."

I watched the shadows in the water a while longer, then we moved on to see some of the springs that create the Williamson. "Are all the springs on your land?" I asked.

"Most, but not all. There's one in the National Forest campground just south of us. You passed it on the way up here."

A fish began rising on the opposite bank. John and Scott took turns casting to it but didn't get a rise.

"Tricky current," I said. "Slow water next to the bank, but fast current between. Makes it hard to get a drag-free drift."

"We've got good fishing," Scott said, "but it's not like going to the trout farm. The better anglers always catch more."

We chatted a while about the ranch's approach to grazing and land management. The Hydes adhere to a holistic resource management philosophy and include fish and wildlife in their decision making. They are ardent conservationists and bird watchers. They've always had an eye for what was best for the land, and that has paid off in ways never planned. Now Yamsi's fish and wildlife are attractions, and paying guests are a significant part of the ranch's income. At Yamsi, the Hydes show how fish and cattle can co-exist, and how trout can help pay the rancher's bills.

"Do other land owners see the benefits of making fish and wildlife part of their ranching strategy?" I asked John.

"Some," he said. "A few are beginning to see the light."

My visit to Yamsi raised two important and related issues: the role of private landowners in fish and wildlife conservation, and fee-based fishing *vs*. public fishing.

Much of Oregon's lands are owned by the federal government, but as anyone knows who has followed the old-growth forest debates and cattle grazing controversies, federal ownership does not mean preservation. All government resources are subject to the political process, and there are some very powerful entrenched interests who want those resources and aren't concerned about the impact on fish and wildlife.

But the Feds don't own it all; private land owners possess much of the state's most productive river habitat. Few individual landowners, however, have the financial reserves to ignore the income potential of resources under their care. Conservationists can preach stewardship until the third millennium, but most landowners have to think about the bottom line. Operations such as Yamsi show that good stewardship can be profitable.

The second issue is a philosophical one and is closely related to the first. Unless landowners charge a goodly sum for access to their property, they have little incentive to accommodate fish. Few anglers can pay $200 a day, and even those that have deep pockets often object to paying for their fishing. The idea of paying for what used to come free sticks in their craw, no matter how big the trout are. And there is the nagging feeling that fee-based fishing can breed elitist attitudes.

Regardless of how one feels about elitism, private fisheries clearly show how good angling could be everywhere—if the land is well tended and the fish are released.

CrystalWood Lodge near the Wood River

Rich McIntyre picked another morel mushroom and put it in a bag. "Two more should do it," he said. The mushrooms would become part of that evening's dinner at CrystalWood, a fly-fishing lodge owned by Rich and his wife Karen. The lodge is an 1890's-vintage farmhouse that was the first homestead in the Upper Klamath basin. It has been remodeled with the tasteful eye of an interior designer. Meals are gourmet, as Rich's mushrooms indicate, and while the ambiance is informal, it's definitely upscale. CrystalWood and Yamsi are both worth the money they charge, but the two are as different as attorneys and cowboys.

Rich stopped for another morel. After putting it in his bag, he pointed out a grove of thick-trunked trees whose yellow leaves rattled in the light breeze. "See those aspens?" Rich said. "We think they're the biggest ones in Oregon." He looked around at the flattened grass. "Elk bed down here. You can see them most mornings.

Fine food, big trees, and elk are not the only amenities at Crystal-Wood. "Our focus is trophy trout," Rich said. "We have access to private water on the lower Williamson as well as Crystal Creek. But most of our fishing is on leased land along the Wood River. We have the largest wild trout you'll ever fish over. Rainbows average eight pounds and reach sixteen. The typical brown trout is 18 inches, but many go much bigger."

"How much bigger?" I had a flashback of a big brown slicing a green wave at Suttle Lake.

"Eight pounds. Ten maybe."

"How hard is it to catch them?" I asked.

"It's not easy," he said. "I'd be misleading you if I said it was. On a good day, you might hook five or six big fish and land two."

"And on a bad day?"

He shrugged. "This is highly-technical spring creek fishing. I've got a staff of five guides, and we do all we can to help our guests find trout. But we're talking about fishing. There are no guarantees."

To provide more reliable angling for his guests, Rich is building two small lakes on his 130-acre property. The lakes will be spring-

Private Fishing in the Klamath Falls Area

Yamsi Ranch. *Yamsi is a working cattle ranch, so guests experience a bit of the "old West" as well fine meals and excellent fishing on the Williamson River. Current rates are $200 per day, which includes fishing, guide, meals, and lodging. There is a three-day minimum stay. Phone: 541/783-2403; write: PO Box 371, Chiloquin, OR 97624.*

Hyde Lake. *This 300-acre man-made lake owned by Yamsi Ranch holds rainbow trout to four or five pounds. If you stay at Yamsi (see above) Hyde Lake comes free, but you don't have to be a ranch guest to fish the lake. One-day access is currently $60, and you can make arrangements through Williamson River Anglers (see below).*

CrystalWood Lodge. *The Williamson River Club at CrystalWood Lodge has private access to sections of the Wood and lower Williamson River, and Upper Klamath Lake is a short hop away. Huge wild rainbow and brown trout are available. CrystalWood Lodge is an old homestead that has been tastefully converted to a luxury resort. Current rates are $195 per day for an angler, $160 for a non-angler; three meals a day are included, as well as lodging. Phone: 541/381-2322; write: PO Box 469, Fort Klamath, OR 97626.*

Horseshoe Ranch. *This working cattle ranch in the Wood River Valley offers six miles of private access to the Wood River, as well as a private lake on the ranch property. Current rates are $200 per day and include river access, lodging, breakfast and dinner; guide service is available. Phone: 541/381-2297; write: PO Box 495, Fort Klamath, OR 97626.*

Williamson River Anglers, *a fly shop on US 97 near Chiloquin, can handle bookings for Yamsi, Hyde Lake, and Horseshoe Ranch. They can also make arrangements for fishing guides and private cabins in the area. Phone: 541/783-2677; write: PO Box 699, Chiloquin, OR 97624.*

Denny Rickards' Guide Service *can be reached at 541/356-2385.*

fed and a couple of acres each. Anglers frustrated by the Wood's wary browns and mammoth rainbows will find easier fishing in them, but no lead-pipe cinches.

"Would you like to try a few casts on the Wood?" he asked me as he stuffed another morel into his bag.

"Twist my arm," I said.

I walked along the Wood to my mile-long "beat," staying well back from the river so as not to alert any trout. My plan was to walk the river bank to the big pine deadfall that marked the extent of my beat, then fish back to the truck.

The Wood is like the upper Williamson: a forty-foot wide spring creek that snakes through open, flat country. Where the upper Williamson runs along a high plateau, the Wood is at the valley floor. It enters Upper Klamath Lake, and that is where the big rainbows come from.

The country was just open enough to make me careless about my backcast, but after retrieving my fly from a few trees, my over-confidence faded. The riparian areas that CrystalWood leases have been fenced to keep cattle out, so the grass is tall. Pines sprout here and there, and willows grow near the bank.

The Wood is mostly shallow, with a silt bottom and moderate flow. Occasionally, the river slows and forms deep pools, and a few areas have weed beds or rocky bottoms. Downed trees sometimes angle into the river, hissing in the current and creating small whirlpools. There are also undercuts in the banks, especially on the river's frequent bends.

These structural changes create lairs for big trout, but also many places in which to snag a fly. I had begun by casting a huge, white rabbit-fur streamer Rich had given me (the fly was so big that I think the tyer used an entire rabbit on it), but it soon became a casualty

I switched to a Matuka, quartering it downstream and working it into the dark niches and tangled waters that might hold trout. A hatch would be nice, I thought—some mayflies or caddis that would encourage the trout to reveal themselves. But I have fished enough hatches on rivers like this to know that even actively feeding fish would not guarantee success. Rich was right: this is technical fishing, and five or six fish with only two landed would be a good day.

It was a pleasant two hours for me, but only because of the sunny fall day and the beautiful river. No huge rainbows blessed me with a grab, no gape-mouthed browns chased my streamers. But I could imagine it.

That night I phoned Denny Rickards and asked what time to meet him the next morning for fishing the lake.

"Forget it," Denny said. "This cold snap killed the fishing. I've been out there two days in a row and only had one good fish."

He waited for my reply, but I was still mulling over this news. One more fishery shutting down for the season. It was that time of year.

"We could still go out if you'd like," he said, "but I think it's done for the year. All you'll get is cold hands. This lake can be so good, I'd hate for you to fish it when it's bad."

I thought about the cold day on the lower Williamson, the frost on the bushes, the ice in the guides. My toes.

"Thanks," I said. "I'll call you in the spring."

15

Slow Flies, Fast Fish

October, Crane Prairie Reservoir

On crisp October nights, as the north wind skittered leaves across the patio, I lay in bed and dreamed of fish. I saw bright summer steelhead layered along the lava ledges of desert rivers, salmon swelling tea-colored coastal creeks, and brown trout slicing through green waves in mountain lakes. But most of all I dreamed of deep-bellied rainbows cruising the ancient stream beds of Crane Prairie Reservoir.

More than any other fish, these out-sized trout had evaded me all year. On my five trips to Crane Prairie, I'd been frozen in May, frustrated in July, sunbaked in August (twice), and thwarted in

September. A few trout had come to my fly; the biggest was a mere 18 inches, about two-and-a-half pounds. But I'd seen none of the fat five and seven pounders which roamed the lake and haunted my dreams.

I was not alone in defeat. Every Crane Prairie fly fisher I knew seethed with blighted hope. The usual hatches had not come off, the trout had not concentrated where expected, it had been too hot, too cold, too windy, and too calm. Nothing had happened as expected, and most of the lake's anglers had given up. I took a deep breath and ventured to Crane Prairie for a few last, desperate casts into a sea of frustration.

I arrived about noon. Brilliant autumnal sunshine was yielding to high haze—and wind. Although it was warmer than my trip to the Williamson, it was still in the low forties, and I could easily imagine that if it clouded over it might snow. And that first snow would instantly close the roads and bring an end to the fishing in the Cascade Lakes until spring. This was the end of the line, and if Crane's big rainbows were going to appear at the end of *my* line, they had to do it in the next two days.

I slid the Klamath off its trailer at the main campground, a huge Forest Service facility that sports over 130 campsites. The lake had dropped since my last visit, and my eight-horse Mercury clunked the bottom a few times as I motored into the Deschutes channel. Anglers seemed to disagree on the state of the weather. I saw everything from shorts and T-shirts to thick sweaters and yellow rain slickers. There was more consensus on the fishing—few trout had been caught, or at least few were admitted to.

At the other end of the lake I got similar responses from anglers in the Rock Creek area, off Quinn channel, and in the Cultus channel. I fished a while at each stop, but hooked nothing and saw nothing hooked by others. The wind worsened, and I headed back to the relative quiet of the lake's east end, which, although it is the windward shore, has enough standing snags to break the waves.

Nature called, and before settling down to some serious fishing, I nosed the boat into a cove. The cove was shallow, and when the Klamath ground to a halt I was left with a ten-foot walk through ankle-deep water to get to shore. I climbed out and tried to tightrope along some waterlogged branches. You know the expression about falling off a log? I proved (again) how easy it is and found myself standing in water over the tops of my shoes. That's when I noticed the boat drifting away. Relieved of my weight, it was no longer grounded and the wind had caught it. I waded deeper and pulled the boat to shore. I was now wet halfway to my knees.

Eventually, I got back onto the lake, but my socks and shoes where soaked. I took them off and put them in the sun to dry. Despite the cool temperature, my bare feet stayed warm as long as I kept them in the sun and off the boat's aluminum floor.

Finding a quiet spot, I anchored the Klamath and looked around. It was an undistinguished location, one I'd rarely fished before, but the channel turned here, and I am a big believer in fishing channel turns. When Crane Prairie dam was built, it backed up the Deschutes River and flooded a broad plain. The original riverbed is still there, however, and like most riverbeds, it has deep places on the outside of its bends. When Crane Prairie warms or the lake level drops, trout concentrate in the channels, especially in the deeper spots where it turns.

As I surveyed the water, a rise appeared. Then another. They could have been after caddis or midges or mayflies. When I don't know what's going on at Crane Prairie (which is often), my standard approach is to tie on a size 10 olive Woolly Bugger. I rummaged through the fly box and picked one at random. I tied the fly to an 18-foot leader tapered to 3X and fastened to an intermediate line—my standard rigging for Crane Prairie.

I cast near a rise and slowly retrieved the fly. (At Crane Prairie, a slow retrieve is essential; if your retrieve isn't driving you nuts, it's too fast.) Half the line was back in the boat when I felt a slight "stickiness." I tightened, and the line went taut and zipped across the water. Five minutes later, a fat 18-inch rainbow was released back to the lake.

It was fun, and I would never diminish the sport that Crane's medium-sized fish can give a fortunate fly fisher. The 16-20 inch trout are the most common, and—inch for inch—the best fighters. But I still wanted a big fish.

I cast some more, and a 13-inch rainbow came to me. Mindful of the stress a fish can put on a knot, I retied the fly. I'd hate to go through all this effort, then lose a big fish because of a weak knot. Rises continued on my right, but off to the left I saw a different kind of rise, the kind that leaves a bubble the size of a softball. The kind of rise made by a really big fish.

It was just beyond my casting range, so I quietly raised the anchors and used the electric motor to move 30 feet closer. I carefully re-anchored, letting the rope slip smoothly through my hands. I looked for the fish, but it was no longer rising. I waited a few more minutes, and there was a plooop, and one of those softball-sized bubbles lay on the surface. I waited out a few more rises, then cast.

He took it.

Line ripped through the water, the reel made its mad-duck noise, and the rod bent and throbbed just like it did in my dreams. The fish ran, came in, ran again, stayed fifty feet out and shook its big head. It came slowly to the boat until the leader knot was just past the tip of the rod. I could see the rainbow clearly, a big heavy-bodied male around five pounds. He was just ten feet from my hand. They always have another run after they get close like that, so I didn't force him. He ran again, came reluctantly back, and once more the leader knot neared the rod tip. Then the rod bounced with a sudden release of tension, and the trout swam slowly away.

I was gutted. All I wanted was to touch it, to count coup on a fish that had eluded me for months. I checked the Woolly Bugger. No failed knots, no bent hooks. Somehow, the fly just pulled loose. It happens.

I kept casting. In an hour and a half I hooked ten fish and landed four. The fish I landed were all between 13 and 18 inches. It was a poor ratio of landings to hookings, and I'd lost the biggest fish, but it was still a whale of a lot of fun. And I'd done it all barefooted.

The wind came up, and my anchors began to drag. Casting became dangerous, so I headed farther east, where I found shelter but no fish before sunset.

Fishing the Channels of Crane Prairie

If you want to understand one of the keys to fishing Crane Prairie, take a hike along the Deschutes River above the lake. In summer, it's a pleasant walk with lots of wildflowers and not a few mosquitoes, but the important thing to notice is the character of the river. It is just a creek at this point, barely 30 feet across. Mostly it is shallow water, but there are deep places on the outside of some bends, and every once in a while the river slows into a deep pool. That same structure exists in Crane Prairie Reservoir.

When the dam flooded the ancient prairie, the old creek and river beds were still there. When the water warms or drops, trout gather in these channels in search of deeper or cooler water and the food that collects there. And within the channels they will favor the deeper holes that existed in the old streambeds—the outside bends and deep pools. Sometimes the holes are only a foot or two deeper than the rest of the channel, so they can be difficult to find. But once you locate one, mark well how to find it again because you've discovered the El Dorado of trout.

Knowing where a depression lies is not enough, however. To fish it well you have to approach quietly (oars or electric motor only), then carefully position your boat and anchor silently. You need to be as far away as your casting skill will allow. Cast carefully so as not to spook the trout, and sometimes give the water a rest of at least half an hour.

I returned to my camp at Hosmer Lake. It was Sunday night, and a few die-hards were still in the campground. I knew none of them and ate my supper alone. In mid-October, the sun is long gone by 6:30. Not only does the light go, but at this altitude it chills quickly. When the last dinner dish was put away, it was near freezing. I started a campfire, and it added cheer, heat, and enough light to read a book, but I didn't stay up long. At 9:00 I crawled into the tent and dreamed again of big trout.

"It was the most fun I ever had with my shoes off!" I told Jim Dexter.

"Really?" he said, with a cocked eyebrow.

"Well, with my shoes off and my pants on," I said. "Ten fish in an hour and a half. For me, that's good fishing on this lake."

Jim is the owner of Dexter's Fly Shop in La Pine. Monday is his day off, and we had made arrangements to fish together, or as together as you can be when you are in separate boats. Jim has fished here for decades and knows the lake far better than I, so I was glad for his company and guidance.

"Put your boat here," Jim said quietly, looking around to make sure no one was within earshot. "No, not there. Here." He pointed to a spot ten feet from where I was about to release the anchor. "Yeah, there. Now anchor."

I did as I was told and rigged my rod. The morning was raw, but bearable. Gray clouds hung low, covering the mountain tops, and the wind blew in fitful gusts. It was cool, but warmer than yesterday.

Jim stood in his small aluminum pram and pointed with his rod. "See down there by that snag? Ten feet this way, there's a log on the bottom. The big ones hang out just this side of it. Put your fly past it, then retrieve. Slowly. And try one of these." He handed me a bead-bodied fly with an orange hairwing.

Jim is a master fly tyer and constantly tinkers with new patterns, especially for lakes. When he hands me a fly, I use it. And catch fish on it. The Woolly Bugger was still fastened to my tippet, however, and I was eager to start, so I saved Jim's fly for later.

I cast to where he pointed. It was a long reach, and my fly consistently landed ten feet short. It would have been no problem for Jim. He can cast farther into a headwind than most people can cast in a flat calm. But he had given me the best water, and although I didn't deserve it, I was grateful and wanted to make the most of it.

"Should I move closer?" I asked.

"No. They'll spook."

I kept at it, but was still short. After a few minutes, my line tugged taut. An 18-inch rainbow came in and was admired, then released. I decided to try Jim's fly. After a few casts, the wind died just enough to give me a break, and the fly dropped into the prime fish zone. I waited a couple of seconds, then began a slow retrieve.

The water exploded.

The six-weight Sage rod jerked in my hands. I could feel it bend clear into the cork grip. Line raced off the reel, and the water exploded again as a huge rainbow leapt into the air and landed with a crash. My mental scale gauged the fish: seven pounds, easy.

"Nice fish," Jim said calmly from his boat. "Probably around five pounds. Maybe six."

Jim is conservative about these things. I knew it was at least seven pounds. But I had no time to argue because the trout was on another run, taking me into my backing.

Line slowly came back onto the reel. The trout was within forty feet of me when it made another slashing run. And the rod went limp.

I reeled in, expecting to find I'd been broken off, but, as had happened yesterday, the hook had pulled out. I clipped off the fly, put it in the palm of my trembling hand, and passed it to Jim, who had brought his boat near mine.

"Take a look at your fly," I said. It was shredded, stripped bare of all but one bead and a few scraggles of orange hair.

Jim examined it. "Yeah," he said fondly, "some days they like these."

Unlike yesterday, I was not gutted by the loss of another big trout. I had a feeling about this day, that it was going to be good. The morning had hardly begun, I knew where fish were, and they were active. I was going to have great fishing. Further, I was convinced I deserved it. This latter point was the most important, more critical than choosing the right fly. I had paid my dues on this lake, and the trout owed me—big time. I tied the Woolly Bugger back on and cast some more.

Again, the water exploded.

This fish was a five-pounder, not as large as the other but big enough. As it came near the boat, the top section of my four-piece rod came off and slid down the leader until the tip-top rested against the trout's nose.

"Cute," said Jim.

I ignored him. We both knew that if the trout broke off, the rod tip would slip off the end of the leader and be gone. I played the fish carefully with my 9-1/2 foot rod, seven feet of which was in my right hand, and 2-1/2 feet of which was tickling the nose of a very large rainbow.

I was lucky, and the fish came to me. I don't usually use a net, but this time I scooped up the trout and quickly retrieved the rod tip. We took some photos and let the fish go. Then I went after more trout, and I found them.

By noon, I had hooked seven fish and landed six. All were between three and five pounds, and four were over four pounds. That's my reckoning. Jim put them at a pound less, but I've measured a lot of fish, and I believe him to be stingy with piscatorial poundage

Not only had I landed some big trout, but I seemed to be the only one catching anything. Even Jim had only one good fish, but of course he had given me the best water. He was now anchored 200 feet away from me and was casting to a big rainbow that was working the area. He had a pluck but no hookup, and finally said he had to go.

"I thought you'd be here all day," I said. "I was planning to treat you to dinner at South Twin." I'd been looking forward to a good meal at Twin Lakes Resort's fine restaurant. I wanted to do something for Jim, and besides, I was tired of my own cooking.

"Can't." Jim said. "I'm taking care of my boy this afternoon." He pulled up the anchor and started his motor. "Don't forget about this big fish here." He looked at the water he'd been casting to. "I'm leaving him for you."

Jim headed for shore, and I resumed fishing. The day had warmed into the high forties, but the wind was getting worse. I decided to rest the water we had been fishing all morning, and headed out for a look at other parts of the lake. They proved too windy, so I returned to the Deschutes channel.

As I neared the spot I'd fished yesterday, I decided to give it another try. I anchored in choppy, whitecapped water, braced myself against the rolling boat, and cast. Ten feet of line came in before there was a solid grab, and another fish came to my hand. A few more casts brought yet another. I'd have stayed, but the anchors were dragging. I left and searched for gentler water.

I anchored in the spot Jim had left and watched the other anglers before beginning to fish. A few were still about, but none looked as satisfied as I felt. I only saw one fish caught, a 12 incher. As near as I could tell, I was having wonderful fishing while a lot of other anglers had little to shout about. I cannot overemphasize how rare an event that is.

I made a few casts and soon felt resistance to my retrieve. The line tightened then lifted from the water as the rod bent to the weight of another big rainbow. This one leapt high, a silver quivering thing. It came straight up from the water and showed me its fat profile, then landed with a noise that turned heads three boats away. Like the others, it was deep-bellied and strong shouldered, a healthy, well-fed trout—yet another five-pounder coming eagerly to my fly.

By day's end, I'd hooked twelve fish and landed ten. All were over three pounds, and several were a good five. By the standards of Crane Prairie's ace fly fishers, that was a good day, but not a great day. For me, it was wonderful, and my pleasure was sweetened by the sure knowledge that I deserved every fish that came to my fly, and maybe even a few more.

Over a day and a half, I'd hooked 22 big rainbows, and 20 of them had been on the same olive Woolly Bugger. I examined it to see if there was anything special about it. I saw nothing that distinguished it from any of the dozen size 10 olive Woolly Buggers that occupied a bin in my fly box. Peas in a pod are more distinctive from each other. As I put away my gear, I clipped off the fly and saved it for the Woolly Bugger Hall of Fame.

The fishing had been outstanding, but something was missing from this trip to Crane Prairie: the birds. A few eagles hung around (the local population actually increases in the winter), and an occasional goose or crane could be heard, but the osprey had left for their winter range in Central America. I missed their shrill kree-kree and the sight of them circling overhead, hovering, dropping with a smack to snatch another unwary fish.

Osprey weren't the only ones who felt the approach of another mountain winter. When I drove to Twin Lakes Resort, I found it closed. They, too, had gauged the cold west wind and, knowing a blizzard could hit any day, had closed two weeks early. I couldn't blame them.

I traveled an empty road to my camp at Hosmer. Everyone had left, and the campground was dark and deserted. No light shone but mine. The only voice was the wind in the trees, and unlike its summer voice, which welcomes and soothes, it spoke of harsh winters and invited me to leave.

Still, I lingered. I built a fire and cooked my dinner by its light. The burning wood cast a ten-foot circle of warmth and cheer, but beyond its yellow flicker I could see a solid wall of darkness and cold. Soon—maybe tonight—snow would blanket this camp, and the lakes would be enshrouded with ice. Trout that I'd sought for half the earth's solar transit would lie beneath the frozen surface in a state near hibernation. Did they dream of summer hatches as I dreamed of trout?

I had intended to stay another day, but I knew when I didn't belong. I struck the tent, packed it in the truck, and doused the fire. My headlights cut a path through the night as I took to the road and let winter claim the mountains.

16

Tidewater

October, Alsea River Tidewater

By the end of October, fishing opportunities were shutting down everywhere. Sometime soon I would have to cancel a fishing trip because a river was blown out. That event would mark a transition into "winter" fishing, when steelhead and desert trout are the primary options.

We had not yet reached that point, but it didn't take a prophet to see that it was coming soon. A cold drizzle fell every couple of days, and even when it didn't rain, the skies were cloudy and the sun was seldom seen. I was neglecting work and home while I crammed "one last" fall fishing trip into my schedule. This was my second "last trip," and there would probably be one more. Less desperate times would come soon enough, and I could catch up on work while waiting for rivers to drop and clear.

We were well past the equinox, and the sun traversed a lower arc every day. Its light was diffused by ragged gray clouds that hid the peaks of the Coast Range and hung in the valleys like lost sheep. It's a time of year without shadows, when colors fade, and the only natural hues are lead gray and forest green.

At home, I'd cleaned up the last of the leaves from the eight big maples in my yard. Riverside, the alders had also lost their leaves and stood skeleton-like as they waited patiently for their spring resurrection.

I grew up in the Northwest, and I'm seldom depressed by the drizzly, short days of endless gray. However, the weather pushs me inward. Like the trees, I tend to withdraw, looking at such deep-rooted issues as life, death, renewal.

I'd moved my fishing to the coast. Normally, I'd have been pursuing coho salmon, but the runs had been mismanaged for years, and over the last three decades they had crashed to less than 3% of their previous levels. Still, some fish bureaucrats maintained that they'd done well by the salmon, and this downturn was not their fault. Right.

Since the coho were a no-show, I was after fall chinook, and the place I pursued them was tidewater. Tidewater is neither river nor bay, but an area of transition that each river passes through before it empties into the sea. The water is brackish, but more fresh than salt. The walls of the river canyon flatten and spread out, so tidewater feels like being on a wide river, except twice a day the water seems to flow uphill as the flood tide pushes against it.

In the fall, before the rivers have enough water to support fish and fishing, but after the fish have moved out of the saltwater bays, you can find salmon in tidewater. It seems simple: the fish are corralled in a smaller space, so they should be easier to find. Like most things fishy, however, it gets complicated. In the ocean, salmon are

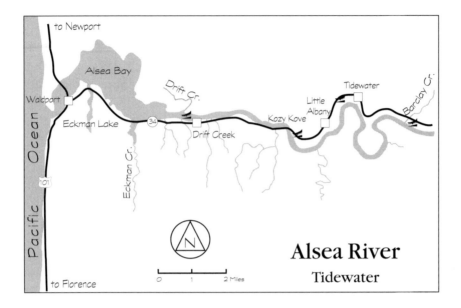

Alsea River

Tidewater

unconstrained and hence less wary; confined in tidewater, they become cautious. In the ocean, salmon are aggressive feeders, but in tidewater they are not. In the rivers, salmon are easily located; in tidewater, they have more places to go, and the water lacks definition.

The result is that tidewater holds super-wary fish that don't like to open their mouths and could be anywhere. In fact, I could build a pretty good case that of all the places to seek salmon, tidewater is the worst.

The Kozy Kove store sits alongside the Alsea tidewater. When I went in to pay my $4.00 launch fee and buy some bait, I asked about the fishing.

"Slowing down," the clerk replied as he handed me my change. "It's not as good as it was."

This response required some thought. To interpret it, one would have to know the starting point. "Slowing down" from what? If the fishing had been red hot, then "slowing down" could mean it was still pretty good, but if the fishing had been poor, "slowing down" might imply a total absence of salmon. It didn't really matter anyway. I'd driven here to fish the Alsea tidewater, and I'd spend the day doing it, regardless of the state to which the fishing had slowed down.

It was near high tide when I launched the Klamath and motored upriver. I asked a few anglers if they had found any chinook, but no one would admit to it. Most of them were either trolling spinners or casting bait-and-bobber rigs. Both tactics work, but bobbers let you reach water you can't get to by trolling.

The main difference between bobber fishing for 40-pound chinook and bobber fishing for 8-inch perch is the size of the bobber. Chinook anglers use a large wooden version through which the line passes. A bit of lead below the float keeps it upright in the water, and a short length of dacron line tied above the float keeps it from sliding up. A sand shrimp or other bait is impaled on a hook about five feet below the float. When in tidewater, chinook often hold in slack water or under overhanging trees. They like snaggy areas, too.

I put together a bobber rig, anchored off a likely place, and cast downriver. Because the tide was flooding, the float came back to me. Line control is important when bobber fishing, and for this reason many anglers use a floating dacron line rather than monofilament. Monofilament sinks, and the current will make it bow, which drags the float in an unnatural way. Float fishing is a lot like drifting a very big dry fly, and in both cases you want a drag-free drift.

Long drifts are desirable when fishing like this because too many casts will spook the fish. On the other hand, you shouldn't make casts so long you can't control the line. As the float comes back, you have to prevent the line from dragging, and you also need to reel in so there is just a little slack. If there is too much slack line, you can't strike quickly if a chinook takes your bait.

I'm hardly a bobber expert, but it seems to me that if there is a drawback to the technique it's the size of the float. It's a big thing, and it makes quite a ruckus when it lands. Big floats are needed because chinook rods are stiff and can't cast a light rig.

As I fished, I wondered if an English carp rod with a small balsa float would be a better tool. Carp rods are long (12 feet), so you can more easily control the line and keep the float from dragging. They can cast light-weight tackle with accuracy and distance, and they can handle forty-pound fish. Maybe in another decade tidewater anglers will be using carp rods for chinook.

That would be a shock to the old timers, of which there are plenty on salmon waters. There's something about salmon, especially chinook, that brings out the old guys. I think it's because chinook, coho, and steelhead were the species of choice with Northwest anglers for decades. When the runs were relatively healthy—and not too many years ago they were—people flocked to the coastal waters in the fall and, compared to today, had an easy time catching big salmon. Many anglers grew up fishing this way, and salmon became their primary prey. Declining runs have forced younger anglers to branch out to trout, lake fishing, walleye, sturgeon, and other species, but the old guys always show up for the salmon.

I don't mean to imply that salmon fishing is a geezer sport, because it isn't. On the other hand, you see a lot more gray-haired folks hanging onto chinook rods than you see flipping flies on the Deschutes.

Not all gray-haired anglers are sitting on the bank or running a boat, though. I saw one bewhiskered fellow swimming in the water looking for salmon. He was a harbor seal. I figured he wasn't going to encourage any chinook to come out and grab my bait, so I headed upstream. I tried several different spots, but there were no takers in any of them. Coming around a bend, I saw a boat in mid-river with a fish on. After a brief fight, the occupants netted a buck around 30 pounds.

"Seen any more?" I asked.

"Only this one," one of the anglers said. "I heard about another one earlier this morning."

It was becoming increasingly clear what the store clerk meant by "slowing down." A few fish were around, though, and I poked my float in various coves and backeddies, but I had no more success than before. Farther up, I saw a chinook roll in a small backeddy overhung with alder branches. The tide had turned and was now ebbing, so I cast upriver and let the float drift into the eddy, circle around, then drift out. I thought it bobbed a little on one pass, but whatever disturbed it didn't come back, and after a few more minutes of casting I moved on.

Coming around a bend, I saw the head of a big chinook on the bank about five feet above the high-tide line. Most of the body was gone, but I estimated it must have weighed 35 pounds when intact. A seagull was picking at the remains. It hadn't been there long because the fish's eyes—usually the first thing to go—were still staring at the world.

I wondered how it got there, and what had consumed the rest of it. Then I remembered the seal I had seen earlier. Seals take a few of these fish, but not nearly as many as some anglers think. Seals and salmon lived side-by-side for millennia, and each did quite well. It's only been in the last century that we've screwed things up so badly that seals could seriously impact a few salmon runs. When thousands of salmon came in at the same time, they had safety in numbers because the seals could only take so many, and the rest escaped. As the salmon numbers dwindle toward zero, seals take as many fish as they used to, but it's a larger percentage of the run.

Some anglers think seals should be shot because they prey on salmon. The problem, however, is not too many seals, it's too few salmon, and the seals didn't cause the decline. If you carried the seal-shooting argument to its logical conclusion, anglers would train their rifle sights on loggers, ranchers, politicians, dam builders, commercial fishermen, farmers, road builders, hatchery managers . . . and each other.

On the side of the river where houses had not been built, the shore was thick with grass, briars, alders, and ferns. Farther up the bank, fir trees rose until their crowns disappeared into low-hanging clouds. Mist and rain are constants here, and even when moisture isn't falling from the sky, it's seldom sunny, so nothing ever dries out.

The defining qualities of Oregon's tidewater are growth and rot. The growth comes from things that love water and shade, such as the alders. But Mother Nature is not satisfied just to grow a few alders here. The trees become the foundation for moss, and every branch is thick with green, spongy plants that take their moisture from the air, not the soil. Even this isn't enough: delicate ferns grow in the moss, and the alder trunks are surrounded by thickets of grass and briars. It's not a place for those anal-retentive types who like Nature to be neat and tidy.

Tidewater is the coast at its most fecund, a mess of growing things. When I come here I'm reminded of two stanzas from an old song about an early Northwest settler:

> *Arriving flat broke in mid-winter*
> *I found it enveloped in fog,*
> *And covered all over with timber*
> *Thick as hair on the back of a dog.*
>
> *I staked me a claim in the forest*
> *And sat myself to hard toil.*
> *For two years I chopped and I labored,*
> *But I never got down to the soil.*

Rot is another attribute of the tidewater regions. Man-made things never last long here; they are soon consumed. Abandoned houses slump into the dirt and are quickly buried in vines. If you leave a board out, it turns gray and slimy, then spongy, then falls apart. Even well-tended houses have the paint sucked out of them in a few years.

Long before the pioneers arrived, the natural economy of the coast was built on a foundation of decay. In Fall, the riverbanks were thick with rotting salmon carcasses, and bears, birds, and other scavengers feasted on the bounty. Crayfish and insects also gorged themselves on the dead flesh, and salmon fry would come later and eat those same insects and crayfish. So, in an indirect manner, baby salmon were sustained by their parents even though the hens and bucks that gave them life died almost a year before the eggs hatched.

It wasn't just dead fish that sustained the riverine community. Floods created backwaters that became nurseries for young salmon and steelhead. Trees fell into the water, and the woody debris nourished aquatic life as well as providing resting and hiding places for fish. Dead fish, dead water, dead trees. It was death that gave life to the river.

The Indians understood the salmon cycle of birth, growth, leaving home young and immature, returning powerful and ready to mate, then creation of a new generation followed by a death that gave life to their progeny. In that cycle, the Indians saw a divine order, the sacred hoop and connectedness of all things.

Where the Indians saw the mysteries of being, whites saw only dead fish, unproductive farmland, and messy trees. They—we—interrupted the cycle, sure in our hearts that technology could produce better fish. It hasn't worked. People keep pretending that salmon hatcheries can sustain the old runs, but they've never worked beyond a few generations of fish.

One of the drawbacks of the hatchery system (one drawback among many) is its failure to put nutrients back into the river. In trying to bring about life without death, we destroyed the salmon and the communities that depended on them.

I wish that when I die, someone would dump my carcass on the river bank. Then I could join the salmon in providing life to others. What the heck, it's just a body. I won't need it anymore, and it might as well do some good.

Better yet, encase my feet in concrete and drop me in a deep pool in the Deschutes. In time, I'll become part of every trout and steelhead in the river, and when the osprey cries, I'll be there, too.

It won't happen, of course. For one thing, human bodies decay more slowly and disgustingly than fish. Besides, there are laws about that sort of thing, and that's as it should be in these days of too many people and not enough wilderness. Nobody wants to drift the Deschutes and see a bunch of cadavers waving in the backeddies like eelgrass in the estuary, so the rivers will have to live without me.

You are getting morbid and bizarre, I told myself. You're here to catch fish. Live ones. I shook off the introspection and returned downriver to where I'd seen a salmon roll an hour before. I was just in time to see an angler net a 25-pounder from the same water.

For a while, I fiddled around in the area, drifting my float through little backeddies, casting under the white, skeletal limbs of leafless alders. At last the bobber went down and I struck, but did not meet the resistance I expected. The stiff rod still bent, but not much, as I brought in a 13-inch searun cutthroat.

I'd brought a six-weight fly rod as well as my ultralight spinning rig, and spent the rest of the day casting for searun cutthroat. Unlike salmon, searuns don't die after spawning. They come into the rivers in fall, spawn, and leave again in early spring. They repeat the trip several times in their lives. You rarely find a dead searun on the bank, so they don't carry the morbid undertones of fall chinook. I spent the rest of the day casting into slack water with the fly rod and thinking about spring.

Saltchuck and Skookumchuck

Early November

I recently attended a wedding reception in Seattle. The party was in a restaurant that overlooked one of the city's ubiquitous yacht basins, and I spent a lot of time looking out the window at the sailboats, cabin cruisers, and bridgedeckers.

"Do you own a boat?" one of the guests asked me.

"Yes," I said. "I have 43 feet of boat."

"My," she said, fingering the pearls that wrapped her neck. "That's a big boat."

"Actually," I explained, "it's three boats: a 16-foot driftboat, a 13-foot raft, and a 14-foot skiff. If I were to put them end-to-end, they would stretch 43 feet."

She left, not as impressed as she'd hoped to be.

There was a time in my life when boats were more important than fishing. I came by it naturally: my father was a boat nut. An engineer by training and disposition, he was as dispassionate a man as I ever knew—except when it came to boats. He had a zeal for them, and living in Seattle gave him boundless opportunities to indulge himself. He even ran off to sea when he was fourteen, leaving a note for his mother that read, in essence, "Gone to Alaska. Back later." After the cook chased him around the small freighter with a meat cleaver (twice), he decided against a sea-going career, but boats remained a life-long avocation.

Boats were a shared interest for my father and me, a place where we connected. We tended to go our separate ways and didn't do much together unless it involved boats and, preferably, saltwater.

As I grew up, we went through a succession of sailboats and cabin cruisers, none of them very big or fancy. When the boat of the moment was a cruiser, we'd spend two summer weeks ambling through the San Juan Islands, a sheltered saltwater archipelago north of Seattle.

When we weren't cruising, my father and I often fished together on Puget Sound, usually for salmon. I understand now that he was a poor angler and possessed only the most rudimentary knowledge of salmon fishing. But I also understand that he didn't care. For him, being on the saltwater—or saltchuck, as Seattle's old-timers called it—was all he wanted. Fishing was an excuse to be in a boat; catching was nice, but irrelevant.

I loved to be on the water, too, regardless of how few fish we hooked. The mingling aromas of saltwater and tideflats, the cry of gulls, the workboats that plied Puget Sound, the gentle swells of that inland sea—they soaked into my soul like ink into paper. There was something special about being on saltwater. Maybe it was the sense that you were unbounded, free to go anywhere in the world if you had a good enough boat.

My father was well-read, especially about boats and the sea, and through him I was introduced to the literature of seafaring men: Joshua Slocum and his solo voyage around the world, *Two Years Before the Mast*, the *Mutiny on the Bounty* trilogy, and others. I owned the full set of C. S. Forester novels about the fictional Captain Horatio Hornblower; I read and re-read them until they fell apart. But in all my trips to bookstores and libraries, I never once picked up a book about rivers.

After college I worked in the San Francisco Bay area. Because I lived on a peninsula, I had saltwater on three sides of me. I ached for a boat I could sail on the Bay or moor at Half Moon or Monterey, but I couldn't afford it.

While I was in California, my father retired. Shortly after that, he sold the broad-beamed 22-foot sailboat he'd owned for the last seven years and bought his first non-wood boat, a 28-foot fiberglass sloop. It was in dry storage when he showed it to me at Christmas. A few months later, my father's heart gave out. He never got this last boat into the water.

Two years after my father died, I moved back to the Northwest. Throughout the eight years I lived in California, it had always been my plan to return to Seattle, buy some property near Puget Sound, and get a nice boat that was suitable for saltwater. I fantasized about classic 40-foot bridgedeckers or broad-beamed ketches that could make a run to Hawaii. But when I finally left the Bay Area, it was to settle in Oregon. I could have just as easily moved back to Seattle, but I had a strong intuitive sense that Oregon was were I belonged. Once here, I soon became oriented to rivers. Saltwater rarely entered my thoughts.

In the 19th century, when Indians and whites lived in the Northwest in more equal proportions than now, locals of all races spoke at least two languages: their native tongue and the Chinook Jargon, a regional *patois* that mixed Indian words with English and other languages. There were even Chinook-English dictionaries to help newcomers.

Some of the words and phrases came into general use throughout the region. *Chuck*, for example, is the Chinook word for water, hence *saltchuck*, the Jargon word for saltwater. *Skookum* was another word that old-timers often used. It means full of spirit or powerful, and I remember anglers of my father's generation describing a good fishing lure as *real skookum stuff*. Water could be skookum, and rivers that ran fast or places where there were powerful currents were known as skookumchuck.

At some point in my life my focus shifted from saltchuck to skookumchuck. I used to sail wide waters where you could look to the horizon and imagine the curve of the earth. Now I float narrow canyons, reading the strong, twisting forces of the river—sometimes drifting with them, sometimes pulling against.

Saltwater is expansive, open-ended. It appeals most to an outward-looking heart. Skookumchuck is narrow and deep, like the powerful flows and twists of human thought and emotion.

I switched waters after my father's death. Twenty years later, I wonder if his passing triggered a subconscious change in my thought, a change that was manifested in a shift from saltchuck to skookumchuck. Perhaps. At some point every son has to break loose and seek his own home waters.

Newport

I didn't have an ocean-front motel room; they cost too much, and all I wanted was a good night's sleep, not a view. But when I parked the truck and boat trailer, the sound of the surf reached my ears, and if I faced the onshore wind, I could smell the sea.

I'd returned to the Alsea tidewater and had spent a frigid day searching for a late-arriving chinook, or maybe a searun cuttthroat or two. Most fish had moved upstream, but the river was too low for good fishing. I poked around the tidewater expecting little and finding less.

The weather was against me. A strong east wind was blowing, and that's always bad for fishing. The rivers were low from lack of rain, and cold from near-freezing temperatures. Given the time of year, fishing in tidewater would have been mediocre under optimum weather conditions. With this east wind, I was wasting my time.

My intent had been to fish for two or three days, beginning with the Alsea then moving down the coast to search Ten Mile Lakes for bass. When I reached the motel, I phoned about the bass; someone who worked at the resort had heard about a small fish that was caught last week, but there'd been nothing since. My backup plan had been to troll for coho in the Coos drainage, but after my day on the Alsea I knew that was pointless.

I spent a fitful night in the motel. My plans for this trip were inoperable, but I didn't have any alternatives. Indecision and uncertainty disturbed my rest, and I woke up every twenty minutes. Frustrated and insomnolent, I watched late-night TV for an hour, but even that failed to put me to sleep.

At 3:30 a.m. I suddenly knew what I should do. Four hours later I was standing outside the office of Newport Tradewinds Charter waiting for them to open the door, and by 8:00 I was on a 48-foot boat headed for the ocean.

It was a gorgeous day. Inland, the east wind brought freezing temperatures and cold rivers, but on the ocean it meant quiet seas and stunning, fogless views. The sea temperature was near 50 degrees; not something you'd want to swim in, but a lot warmer than the Alsea had been. Out here, fishing was improved by the east wind.

The charter boat had the ocean-going heft of the bridgedeckers I used to fantasize about. Its diesel engines chugged with authority as we passed under the graceful arches of the Newport bridge, which is probably the most photographed structure on the Oregon coast. Gulls followed the boat for a while, then a few pelicans soared past and gave us the eye. A few miles from the harbor I saw a gray whale. Most of them migrate to Baja, but a few hang around Oregon for the winter. A porpoise slashed through one wave, and the green ocean heaved with long three-foot rollers.

By 8:45 we were a mile offshore and drifting over reefs that should hold rockfish. There was only one other angler aboard, an orchardist from Yakima named John. A lean, sixty-ish man with hands and a face that spoke of a life outdoors, he'd headed for Newport after the apple harvest. Since charter boats require at least two anglers before they'll make a trip, he was glad I'd showed up and rescued him from a day of shopping.

Once over the reef, Rob, our skipper, throttled back the engines, and we dropped our lines into fifty feet of water. The tackle was simple: a stiff rod with a salt-tarnished reel, heavy monofilament line, two plastic bass jigs, a hook baited with herring, and a heavy lead weight.

John and I jigged our rods as the boat drifted. With the engines cut back, I could hear the surf on the shore and watch the waves lift as they neared the broad, sandy beach, the sun catching the wind-blown spray. I have often been to the coast and always enjoy the surf. This was a different perspective, however—watching the waves recede from me, rather than approach.

Rob ran back and forth, busy as a waitress in a diner as he checked our lines, his fish locator, and his GPS. When no fish grabbed our jigs, he moved to a different reef. This time, a few fish came to us. After we'd drifted past them, he revved the engines, spun the boat, and settled over the reef again. "Lines down!" he yelled.

We lowered our lines and soon were into fish. John brought up a double—a rockfish on each jig; then I had one, too. More doubles came, and even a few triples. When we were over fish, it was rare to hook only one at a time. As soon as the rods started to bounce, we'd reel up, swing the fish toward Rob, and he would dump them into two plastic buckets, one for John and one for me.

When I fish, I like to do things for myself, but that isn't the etiquette on a charter boat. Charter skippers want you to get your limit as soon as possible so they can go back to port and stop burning costly diesel fuel. Besides, they know what to do, and most of their customers don't. I was mindful of the fact that with only two anglers, this was not a high-profit trip for Newport Tradewinds. So, as if I were the most ignorant dude on the water, I wordlessly let Rob bait my hook and toss fish into the bucket.

When we stopped hooking fish, Rob would yell, "Lines up!" then position us again over the reef. On the third pass, John's rod went into a semicircle—much too deep a bend for the two- and

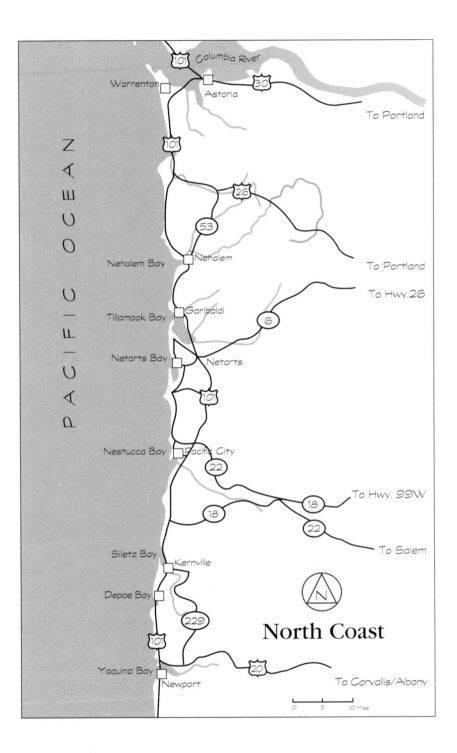

North Coast

three-pound sea bass we'd been catching.

"Ling cod!" he shouted.

I reeled up and watched as John fought his fish. After five minutes, he had it near the boat. It was about twelve pounds, not big as ling cod go, but a good size nonetheless. Ling cod are voracious predators. They have a huge mouth studded with sharp teeth and lie in rocky underwater structures, waiting to ambush unwary fish. When a ling cod takes your bait, you have to play it carefully because they are rarely hooked. They are so greedy that they just hang on tight to the bait until you bring them to the surface. If you lift a ling cod out of the water, it lets go and swims away. John is an experienced ling cod angler, however, and let Rob net the fish for him. He smiled as the fish came onto the boat and said, "I've been doing this for years, and they've always found me a ling."

We continued to re-position over the reef and pick up rockfish. A limit is fifteen each, a point we reached before 11:00. Less than an hour later, Rob was tying up the boat to the charter pier. A young woman with a bucket of sharp knives came and turned my fish into fillets. A couple dozen gulls wheeled over her, begging for scraps, while I checked out the workboats moored nearby and thought about how the day had turned out.

Charter fishing is not my usual cup of tea. It's a meat fishery—production angling where the goal is to fill your bucket as soon as possible—and requires little skill or knowledge on my part. I enjoyed this trip, however. The weather on the ocean was better than anything inland, and the views were clear and luminous. I'd seen a whale and a porpoise and, for the first time in a decade, had felt the Pacific swell under my feet. It was a spontaneous and serendipitous trip, and sometimes those are the ones you remember best.

Before leaving I looked westward through the arch of the bridge to the open horizon, and wondered at the deep currents that had taken me in directions I never planned.

18

Two-Fisted Fly Fishing

January, Sandy River below Oxbow Park

Mark Bachman looked at the bankside willows, some of which were chewed off by beaver, then up at the old growth firs that lined the river's canyon. "People have such big egos," he said. "They think they can improve on this. We've got beaver, elk, deer, otter, bear, coyote. This is wild, this is raw. And it's forty minutes from downtown Portland."

Mark is a fishing guide who works the Deschutes and Sandy rivers. He is also part owner of The Fly Fishing Shop, a retail store on US 26 in Welches. On this foggy January morning we had launched

Mark's driftboat at Oxbow Park on the Sandy, and we would drift seven miles to the takeout at Dabney Park.

Although he is amiable and a delight to fish with, Mark has a deep, commanding voice. An opera fan would call it *basso profundo*, but the rest of the world might think of it as belonging to a drill sergeant. "This is a good run when the water's high," he said, after a short drift. "Start at the boat and work down. It's all good. Fish could be anywhere in the run, so pay attention."

"What fly should I use?" I asked.

He handed me a big red, furry thing. "I call this one 'Big Red.' Start with it. If that doesn't work, try a black one, or switch to a Marabou Spider."

I examined the fly. "It looks like a Rabbit Fur Leech."

"It is, with a few variations."

Over the last few years, I've occasionally fished for winter steelhead with a fly rod and know that the trick is to get the fly down deep, where the fish lie. Usually that means split shot on the leader or a heavy sinking line. In the past, I'd used deep-sinking shooting heads on my eight-weight single-handed rod, but a day of casting the heavy line always left my right shoulder aching. For several years, I'd been thinking that a spey rod—a 15-foot fly rod that you cast with two hands—would solve this problem because it divides the labor. This fall I bought one.

I'd tried it out a few times before today. The first time I used it, I immediately discovered a problem: everything I knew about fly casting was irrelevant. I felt like a beginning fly angler all over again. So I sought out Mark for a day on the river, hoping to find some steelhead, but mostly looking for casting instruction.

Mark is one of Oregon's premiere spey rod advocates. For several winters, he has been taking fly rod steelheaders down the Sandy River and teaching them the rudiments of using a spey rod.

"Form a loop in back," Mark said to me after giving a few pointers.

I cast again and looked back at Mark. "Like that?"

"You'll get there. It just takes practice."

I kept at it, and it got better. A few casts actually looked almost

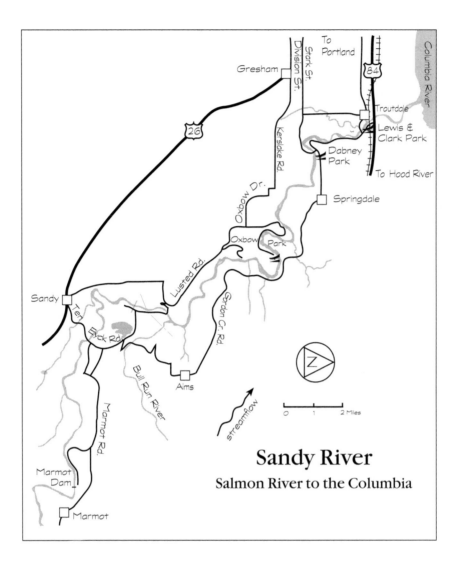

Sandy River

Salmon River to the Columbia

decent. Mark continued to critique and offer suggestions as I cast-step-cast my way through the run. At one point, Mark said, "Richmond, you're a nice guy but you don't listen worth a damn. Now form your loop in *back*."

He was saying something like, "Next time cast over the water, not on it," when the free loop shot out of my hand and the rod went into a deep bend. Eighty feet away, a bright, ten-pound steelhead cleared the water, rushed upstream, then jumped again.

"Fish on!" I yelled. "Yee-haw" I couldn't believe it. A new technique, a run I didn't know, and there was a steelhead on the end of my line. Life can be gooood.

The fly line bowed in the river as the steelhead continued its upstream charge. The fish was into my backing when it headed for mid-river, then made another screaming upstream run.

"Watch the willows," Mark said as the wild hen tired and drifted below me near shore. The river was at its winter level, and submerged willows were in the shallow water waiting to entangle my line as the steelhead twisted and made short runs. The willows were avoided, and the fish came to the beach. Mark took photos, and we briefly admired the silvery, deep-bodied steelhead while reviving it. She left my hand with a splash from her tail and shot back into the river.

"Congratulations," Mark said. "Your first spey-rod steelhead."

Spey rods were originally developed in Britain for Atlantic salmon fishing. In the 19th century, they were made from bamboo and were very expensive. And heavy. At a time when trout rods weighed only four ounces, a bamboo spey rod tipped the scales at a pound and a half. They were brutal rods to use, but the aristocrats who plied them only fished for a short time each day and didn't have much else to do.

In the U.S., early Atlantic salmon anglers used the traditional British spey rod, but shorter, single-handed rods became the vogue a couple of decades into this century. Not only were single-handed rods lighter and less abusive, they were less expensive and better matched to American democratic traditions. Experts like Lee Wulff propounded the benefits of shorter, lighter rods, and spey rods fell into disuse among American anglers.

West coast steelhead fly fishers grew up using single-handed rods. Until recently, few had even heard of spey rods. Nearly all the fly fishing was for summer steelhead, which are often smaller than their winter brethren and will readily move to a fly fished from a floating line. A good eight-weight single-handed rod was a perfect match to the fish and the techniques used to catch them.

While a few die-hards kept casting through the winter, their success was limited. A few experimenters kept at it, and tackle makers such as Jim Teeny began producing fast-sinking fly lines designed for winter steelheaders. At the same time, graphite technology allowed rod makers to build powerful spey rods that weighed less than nine ounces.

Harry Lemire, a steelhead ace from Washington state, experimented with combinations of sinking and floating lines that could be used on a spey rod. He developed a "launcher" system that used a modified weight-forward floating line with interchangeable sink tips. Each tip sinks at a different rate, so an angler can match the tip to the depth and speed of the run being fished.

With graphite spey rods and high-tech line systems, fly fishing for winter steelhead became pleasurable and productive, as I had just demonstrated to myself by bringing a ten-pound wild steelhead to the beach in January.

Mark moved the boat across the river so I could fish the same run from the other side. "Where do you find winter steelhead?" I asked as he rowed.

"In the same kind of water as summer fish," Mark said. "But in winter, that kind of water is in a different place than you find it in summer because the river levels are different. And you need to make some allowance for lower water temperature, which affects the steelhead's metabolism. Under most conditions, your typical winter steelhead will readily move 12 inches up, or 18 inches either side of where it lies. If your fly's farther away than that, there's much less chance that the fish will move to it." We neared the shore and Mark dropped the anchor. "One kind of water I look for is 'tube' water," he said as he climbed out of the boat.

"Tube water?"

"You know, fast on both sides, slow in the middle. Steelhead like to hold in water like that because they can rest in the slow stuff, but if danger comes, they zip into the fast water and let the current carry them away fast."

"I look for water with a sense of quiet anticipation," I said, describing my favorite kind of steelhead water.

"Huh? What's that mean?"

I'm used to this kind of response. Finding the right kind of water is the most important thing a steelheader can do, but few of them can describe the process to anyone else. Every steelheader I've met has his or her own way of describing what they look for. One describes his favorite runs as *transition water*. A little probing reveals that this means runs where the current makes a transition from fast to slow or shallow to deep. Another angler says he looks for water with *definition*, meaning it has the kind of structure, such as rocks or ledges, where steelhead like to hold. My description of "a sense of quiet anticipation" doesn't describe the water at all, but my reaction to it when I see it, a reaction based on having caught a steelhead in similar-looking water in the past.

I'm not sure which description I'd use for the next run I started fishing, but my line went tight on the very first cast. It happened so fast Mark didn't even have a chance to critique my casting.

This fish ran hot for a while, but tired quicker than the first steelhead. When it came to the sandy beach, the reason was clear. Mark ran a finger along the fish's belly. "See that groove?" he said. "This fish is bright and in good condition, but it's already spawned and is headed back to the ocean."

"It's not a wild fish, either," I said. "It's ventral fin has been clipped."

After releasing the spawner, I finished the run, then we drifted down and cast through a few more good spots. At noon, Mark stopped on a sandy beach and whipped up a hot lunch of barbequed New York steak, baked beans, and salad—a welcome relief from my usual peanut butter and jam. I leaned back in the lounge chair Mark had set up; this having-a-guide-do-everything-for-you was something I could get used to. I thought about the wild hen I'd hooked in the morning, and that prompted a question. "Is the wild run healthy in the Sandy," I asked.

Some of Mark Bachman's
Favorite Winter Steelhead Fly Patterns

Steelhead Bunny, (a.k.a. Big Black, Big Red, Big Purple)
Hook: TMC 9394, number 2
Body: Palmered rabbit strip (red or black or purple) over nickel
hook, spaced to let the hook show through for ribbing.
A 3/16 brass head is often slid onto the hook for weight.

Silvey Prawn
Same as Steelhead Bunny, but large eyes are attached at the hook
bend, and feelers made of Super Hair are added. A golden pheasant
tip is wound on behind in back of the eyes and near the eye of the
hook for legs. A golden pheasant rump or flank feather is tied flat on
top for the back of the prawn. Colors vary, but orange is common.

Marabou Spider
Hook: TMC 7999, number 2/0
Hackle: Two marabou plumes wound as hackle with Flashabou be-
tween them. Red over orange with gold Flashabou works well. Other
good choices: hot pink over orange or mixed with gold Flashabou;
purple over dark lilac with purple Flashabou; black over over navy
blue with blue and silver.

Sandy Candy
Hook: TMC 7999, number 2
Pink and orange schlopen or marabou palmered together with or-
ange in front. Gold Flashabou added in middle.

"Some years are better than others," Mark said. "That's only natural. But the runs appear stable, at least for now. The Sandy is the
least dammed of any major Columbia River tributary, and it enters
the Columbia downstream from Bonneville Dam. So at most, the
only major barrier is Marmot Dam, upstream from us." Mark ladled
some more baked beans onto my plate. Steam rose into the cool,

overcast day. "It helped," he said, "that the Sandy was the first river in Oregon to get 'wild and scenic' status, so there's been some protection. Also, the gradient is steep enough that it clears quickly, so natural spawning isn't ruined by siltation. There's so many good things going on, that if wild fish can't recover here, they're doomed everywhere else."

Mark went on to explain that the Sandy River headwaters get over 100 inches of rain a year, so there's lots of fresh water renewing the river. Frequent heavy flows churn up and redistribute the river bottom, so the spawning gravel is continually refreshed. Besides winter steelhead, the river supports spring and fall chinook and summer steelhead. There is not a month when fresh anadromous fish don't enter the river.

Not all the Sandy's fish are wild, however. Both salmon and steelhead are stocked, but only the steelhead are fin-clipped. "If we fin-clipped all the fish stocked in this river," Mark said, "then the regulations could require the release of wild, non-clipped salmon as well as steelhead. The way it is now, people kill wild salmon. And a lot of salmon and steelhead smolts are killed by people who think they're trout. I hate to think how many wild smolts end up on a dinner plate."

Mark looked around at the canyon. Not a house was in sight. The naked limbs of alders were brown against the dark green firs. An eagle turned circles in the gray sky. "You could think you were in a remote part of British Columbia down here," he said. "And Portland airport's a half hour away. We've got to take care of this place."

Protecting the Sandy is one of Mark's passions. He's worked hard to learn the river and its history, and to find ways to improve conditions for its wild fish. He's in a constant battle against those who see only "real estate" and "potential," not what is already there and needs saving. The opponents of wild fish and wild rivers are tenacious and well-funded. "Anyone who thinks this canyon is protected forever has their head in the sand," Mark said as he put away the stove. "If we don't take a tough stance on every issue, we'll lose. Forever."

After lunch, we sat for a few minutes before fishing again. Mark told me about growing up in northern Idaho. "You remember that movie, *A River Runs Through It?*" he said. "All my friends were like the younger brother. Tough. There were six of us that ran around together. Four of them died violently. Two were Marines killed in combat, one in Viet Nam and one in Central America. One was killed in a knife fight in California." He thought for moment, then said, "I forget how the fourth guy died."

As we finished the day's drift, my spey casting slowly improved. No more fish graced the end of my line, but I'd had such a good morning I didn't care. I'd landed two steelhead on new gear, and experienced a wilderness river close to home. I felt renewed, and came back with a firmer resolve to keep this place wild. It won't be easy. You have to be tough to convince people to leave something alone, and you need to keep a two-fisted grip on what is precious.

19

Btfsplk

February, the town of Coquille

The roar grew louder until it filled the dark room, then it faded for a while, only to return a minute later. The noise came from torrential rain, driven by gale-force winds. The rain hammered my motel room until I could no longer sleep. Then a new sound added its voice, a noise like the approach of a jet plane. It rumbled variably, and I was puzzled until I recognized it as thunder. It repeated itself again and again, and my stomach tightened at each long peal.

My gut reaction had little to do with fear of lightning storms. It came from the realization that I had gambled on the weather and lost.

The previous morning I had left home for an extended fishing trip to Oregon's south coast—Coos Bay to the California border. Although this part of the state has always interested me, I had never fished it. I was eager to explore the Elk and Sixes rivers, the Chetco, and the various forks of the Coquille system.

The weather was against me, however. This year we didn't have winter; we had divine vengeance. It hadn't rained so much since Noah built his boat, and rivers throughout Oregon were constantly high or over their banks. The north coast streams had flooded so often that even the smallest freshet turned them chocolate brown with mud and silt.

I reasoned that the south coast had missed the brunt of the winter storms, so the rivers there would be in better shape. Further, everyone knows the weather gets better the farther south you go. Just look at the weather reports for Brookings, a small town a few miles north of the California border. Always warm, even in winter, Brookings is Oregon's banana belt, and the Chetco, a renowned steelhead and salmon river, flows through the middle of it.

For weeks I'd watched the weather reports, searching for a break in the storms that had wracked the state since November. Near the end of February I thought I saw a glimmer of hope, and I went for it. Tonight's storm mocked that decision.

November through March, the primary gamefish pursued by Oregon anglers is winter steelhead. Most are sought in coastal rivers that are usually either too low and clear for good fishing, or too high and turbid. The steelhead—never plentiful these days—might be in the river, or in the ocean, or most of them might have died as smolts two years ago and only the barest remnant returned.

The odds are so deeply stacked against winter anglers that you have to wonder why they would leave a comfortable home to stand in a freezing stream, testing the limits of raingear and human endurance in pursuit of a fish they're unlikely to catch. The easy explanation—"they're nuts"—doesn't dig deep enough into the soul of the winter angler.

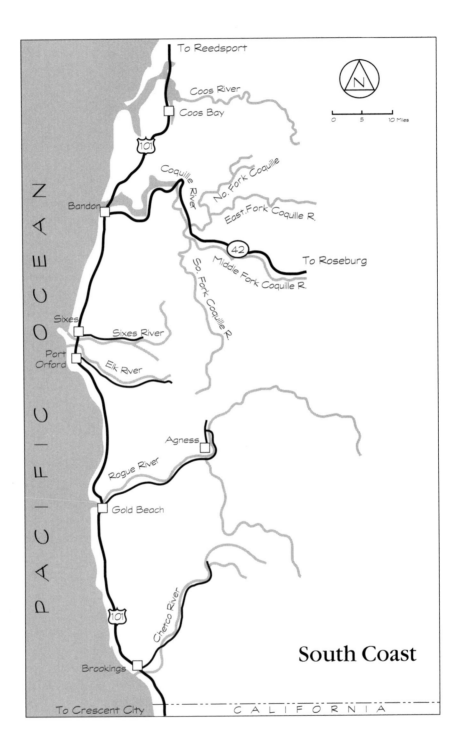

To Reedsport

Coos River

Coos Bay

101

Coquille River

No. Fork Coquille

Bandon

East Fork Coquille R.

42

To Roseburg

Middle Fork Coquille R.

So. Fork Coquille R.

Sixes

Sixes River

Port
Orford

Elk River

Agness

Rogue River

Gold Beach

101

Chetco River

South Coast

Brookings

To Crescent City

CALIFORNIA

PACIFIC OCEAN

N

0   5   10 Miles

To be sure, there are experts who hook at least one fish on most trips. And every now and then you might hit a mild day, cloudy but rainless, when the streams are dropping and have turned that jade color anglers call "steelhead green," and hook three chrome-bright fish before noon. Those days are rare, however, so you have to probe deeper to answer the question, "Why do people do this to themselves?"

One line of reasoning goes like this: Oregon is a great place to live and fish, and some people feel they can't enjoy it unless they first prove themselves worthy. Winter steelheading is one way to do this. It taxes your ingenuity, commitment, knowledge, courage, and faith. If you can keep fishing through a Northwest winter, then your mettle has been tested, and you have earned the right to enjoy yourself. This attitude combines elements of Puritanism with ancient "rites of passage." It fits the traditions of the Oregon Country: it would have been understandable to both the Indians and the religious-minded pioneers who settled the valleys.

For some anglers, however, the winter fishing urge may have even deeper roots: nothing less than the need to demonstrate a victory of the spirit. They go forth in miserable, uncertain conditions, endure the worst that the forces of cold and darkness can fling at them, and thereby attest to the strength and resiliency of the human soul. It is not masochism that makes these Oregon anglers leave a warm hearth for a cold river. They are on a noble quest, spurred by an idealistic compulsion to demonstrate a triumph of hope over despair, faith over cynicism, spiritual strength over physical weakness.

Or maybe they're just nuts.

On my way down yesterday, every stream I passed, from tiny creeks to broad rivers, was high and off-color. If all I had was the evidence of that drive, I'd have said that alders grow in the middle of creeks like mangroves in tropical lagoons, and that the natural color of rivers is brown.

South of Coos Bay, the slough had exceeded its banks and encroached on US 101. When I drove into the little town of Coquille, the mainstem of the Coquille River occupied a portion of state route 42S and all of the city park. When I looked for a motel, I seriously considered its elevation. If the river continued to flood, would it reach my room? I was dragging the driftboat, so I had an escape. However, I didn't think the car insurance company wanted to hear about my new truck being swept out to sea, so I chose a motel on the top of a rise and prepared for the worst.

That night, as the storm beat against my room, it sounded as if the worst had arrived. Lightning, torrential rain, and even hail pounded for a couple of hours, then passed with a final boom of thunder.

North Coquille River

The morning was cloudy but not raining, and I drove to Laverne Park on the North Coquille River, a destination I chose because I'd heard that the North Coquille cleared faster than other branches of the river. This proved true. The North Coquille wasn't exactly clear—it was an olive drab color with about ten inches of visibility— but every other river had the color and clarity of adobe bricks.

The North Coquille is about 60-feet wide and bouldery. It is not boatable, so the only way to fish it is from the bank. Like most other small west-slope streams, its banks are steep and covered with alders and ferns.

I scrambled down the bank and began casting a large, silver-bladed spinner. I had no idea where the good runs were, but in a stream like this, steelhead can be behind any rock with sufficient depth of water. I cast so the spinner would drift near the bottom with its blade turning as slowly as possible. That's the theory, any-way. It's not always easy to achieve, especially when you don't know the water, and I left a few spinners hanging on submerged rocks and tree branches.

To reach each new run I had to climb over, under, or around fallen alders. In some places the banks were steep, and I clung to ferns and tree roots to get by. Once, I tripped on a tree root and sprawled flat. Another time, my feet slipped on the wet soil, and I skidded a few yards downhill on my butt.

At one point, I spied some good looking water, but couldn't figure out how to get to it. A steep, ten-foot wide strip of bare dirt separated me from firmer footing. One misstep and I'd slide straight into the river. I contemplated it for a while, then figured the worst that could happen is I'd get wet. For commitment, I tossed my rod to the other side of the slope. If I fell in, I had dry clothes in the truck. I reached the other side without incident and explored the water with my spinner. You'd think the fishing gods would reward this kind of risk taking. You'd be wrong.

Bank scrambling is normal on small steelhead streams such as this. Though sometimes dangerous, it's good exercise—a lot tougher than those Stair Master things that are so popular with the spandex and sweatband crowd. In fact, some clever person should invent a "Bank Master" exercise machine with programmable slipperiness, tree roots that appear without warning, and a slide that leads to a tub of freezing water. I'd be happy to consult with the inventor.

By noon, I'd covered about a mile of river but remained fishless. I hiked up to the road and headed back to the truck for lunch. At the park, I saw two other anglers sitting on a bench and asked if they'd had any luck. "Hooked two in five minutes," one of them said. "Didn't land either one."

"Where about?"

"Up there. Where the river turns."

I knew from the empty bait containers that littered the bank that this was a popular spot. I'd made a few luckless casts there this morning. Suddenly, the skies opened, and we were deluged with rain. I ducked into the truck and ate lunch. The downpour stopped shortly after I got in the truck. When I was done with lunch and prepared go back to the river, the rain started up again.

This trip was reminding me of the old Lil' Abner comic strip. One of the characters was a gloomy guy who walked around with a cloud over his head. It could be sunny everywhere, but it always rained on him. The character's name was Joe Btfsplk. Al Capp, the comic strip's creator, said "Btfsplk" was his way of spelling a Bronx cheer, the old raspberry. I was beginning to feel like I was Joe Btfsplk.

Showers fell intermittently all afternoon as I fished upstream from the park. The water was suited to a fly rod, so I used the spey rod that had served me so well on the Sandy. I touched no fish, saw no fish, heard of no one catching any fish, and finally gave it up and returned to Coquille.

That night, another storm blasted the coast. I lay in bed and contemplated my options. Tomorrow, the North Coquille would be in no better shape than today. All the other rivers were probably blown out as well. I could at least spend the day exploring, so that when the rivers finally dropped, I'd know where to go.

Elk and Sixes Rivers

A few eons back, big chunks of rock began colliding with the southern Oregon coast. They piled up against each other in a long, grinding collision that bent and broke the rocks. They fused to the mainland, then twisted clockwise as much as a quarter turn. This wrinkled mess of mountains is the rugged southern section of the Oregon coastline. It is as different from the Cascade Range as a teenager's bedroom is from a bank manager's desk.

The Coast Range—the section of mountains along the rest of the Oregon coast—was raised up through a different process, but to a non-geologist, the results look much the same: a rugged jumble of mountains stretching along a north-south line.

Marine currents drive moist air against the coastal mountains, and rain falls as if in a rush to get back to the ocean. Rivulets run down steep slopes and join in the gullies to make creeks. Creeks hurry to the valleys and merge into rivers. Because these mountains are so close to the Pacific, few of the rivers are more than 30 miles long. Further, the mountains are so irregular that the watersheds don't connect. The result is dozens of short rivers leading to the sea, and conditions on one stream do not generalize to its neighbors.

This was clear when I checked out the Elk and Sixes rivers. The Sixes was high and muddy, but the Elk was significantly lower and clearer. Yet the two rivers are sometimes as close as a couple of miles, and are never separated by more than ten miles. The main difference between them is that the Elk watershed has seen less logging and still supports some patches of old-growth forest.

I drove along the Sixes, looking for boat ramps that I could use another day, then moved over to the Elk. Seeking information, I stopped at an RV park and talked to a jovial man with tousled, thinning hair and a stomach that protruded well past his red suspenders.

"A couple of days of no rain, and it'll be good," he said. "There's no point fishing it this high, but if these storms hold off, you'll have fine fishing when the river drops." He fingered his suspenders and looked out at the drizzling sky. "Doesn't look likely, though."

He confirmed my suspicions: even if the sun came out this afternoon, it would be two days before the Elk was in good shape, and most of a week before the Sixes was fishable. I moved on down the road to check out the Chetco.

Chetco River

Clouds hung in the Chetco's deep canyon, and rain occasionally squalled through. This is a big river, often 150-feet wide at this level. The river was high and turbid, but in better shape than the other streams I had seen. Instead of being mud-brown, it was green, and visibility was about a foot. It didn't look like good fishing today, but I could imagine it getting better, maybe as early as tomorrow.

Two major tributaries flow into the Chetco: the North Fork and the South Fork, both of which are closed to fishing. I drove to the confluence with the South Fork and pulled off the road for a closer look. I found a small stick and pushed it into the gravel at the edge of the river. It would serve as a rough gauge of how fast the Chetco was dropping—or rising.

I fixed lunch and ate sitting on the cooler. A car drove up, and two angler-looking men got out and went to stare at the river. I got up and stared with them.

"Kinda high," said the taller of the two.

"Do you fish here much?" I asked.

"Yeah. Here and the Smith."

"How much higher than normal do you think the Chetco is?" I queried.

He scanned the river a bit, tilted his head back, and sighed. "About five feet. If it drops three more feet, fishing could get good. Unless another storm comes in."

After these two left, I retrieved my weather radio from the truck. These handy devices pick up the National Weather Service broadcasts and are a good source of local weather information. I clicked it on but heard only static. Maybe outside the canyon I'd have better reception.

Another rain shower moved through while I put on my waders. I had no hope of hooking a fish but figured I could at least get a little casting practice with the spey rod. There was a gravel bar I could wade to, and a patch of water ran beside it that might conceivably hold a steelhead. I look at it this way: if you're going to practice casting, you might as well do it where there is some small hope of hooking a fish.

After a few dozen casts, three curious otters swam out from the bank and took a peek at me. One of them immediately dove and fled at the sight. I wondered if I really was Joe Btfsplk and the otter had seen the cloud over my head. More likely he saw the 15-foot spey rod and concluded only a dangerous psychotic would carry such a weapon.

The other otters soon became bored with me and went back to whatever they'd been doing before I provided an amusing diversion. Forty minutes of practicing my double spey cast seemed enough, and I waded to the bank. The stick I'd pushed into the gravel revealed that the river was definitely receding. It appeared to have dropped about an inch since I put in the stick an hour ago. I extrapolated that to a three-foot drop by Friday morning, two days away.

It gave hope. Just two days without torrential downpours—two days of no Joe Btfsplk—and the Chetco would be in fine shape for steelheading. It could even provide marginal fishing tomorrow. I decided to stick it out here and not seek other rivers.

I spent the rest of the day checking out river access points and boat ramps. One of those access points is called Nook. It has a boat ramp, and a long bar of heavy cobble stretches downriver for over a quarter mile. Several spots looked to me like good steelhead water, so I decided to return there the next day. I put another stick in the gravel to measure the river's progress, then headed for Brookings and found a cheap motel room.

My plan on this expedition was to stay in motels. The nights are still pretty short in February, and camping in stormy weather didn't sound attractive. It was also my plan to fix my own breakfast and lunch, but eat dinner out. Chinese food held some appeal tonight, so I went into a small restaurant and ordered Kung Pao chicken and hot-and-sour soup.

At the end of the meal, I checked out the fortune cookie. You'd think that in a restaurant a few hundred yards from a major river you'd find a fortune about fishing, something like, "You will find joy and many mint-bright steelhead on the Chetco this Friday." Instead, I got, "Your place is in the driver's seat." Was this a sign that I should go home?

I crumpled up the fortune and dropped it in the leftover soy sauce. My eye was caught by the red wrapper that had covered my made-in-Taiwan chopsticks. I read what it said: "Please try your Nice Chinese Food with Chopsticks . . . the traditional and typical of Chinese glorious history and cultural."

I pondered that the rest of the evening.

While I slept, it rained again. Brookings wasn't quite what I expected in a banana belt. I had picked up a local newspaper after dinner and read in the weather column that Brookings had received over 28 inches of rain in the first six weeks of the year, and over eight inches in the last five days. Then it hit me: bananas grow in tropical rain forests. Apparently, the only difference between Brookings and the rest of the Oregon coast is that the rain is warmer.

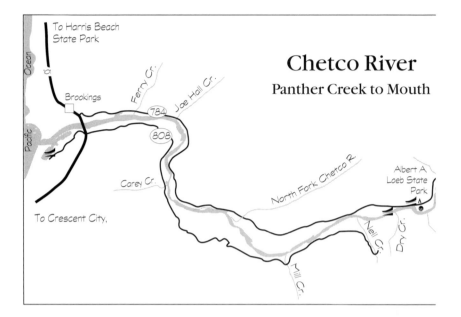

Chetco River
Panther Creek to Mouth

To Harris Beach State Park

Ocean

101

Brookings

Pacific

Ferry Cr.

Joe Hall Cr.

784

808

Carey Cr.

To Crescent City,

North Fork Chetco R.

Albert A. Loeb State Park

Nell Cr.

Dry Cr.

Mill Cr.

But it wasn't warmer that night. When I went to my truck in the morning, the canvas cover over the driftboat was stiff as plywood and sparkled with frost. As I drove up the river, snow splatted on the windshield, and I met several cars with three inches of wet snow on their hoods. Fortunately, the white stuff wasn't sticking to the road.

I stopped first at Nook and checked my stick. The river had dropped a foot and a half overnight, and visibility was a reasonable two feet. My weather radio said there would be scattered showers today, then a big storm would arrive late tomorrow. Thirty-six hours of dry skies was all I needed. The Chetco would continue to fall as I explored it today, and tomorrow I'd be prepared to take advantage of some truly outstanding fishing.

I pushed in another stick at the river's current level and moved up the road to the junction with the south fork. The gravel bar I'd fished from yesterday was now completely exposed. I waded to it and made a few casts out of obligation, but the water was too fast for my fly to get down to the steelhead zone. Unlike yesterday, this was not casting practice. I wanted fish.

The spinning rod would have been the right tool for the job. I thought about retrieving it from the truck, but then decided to stick

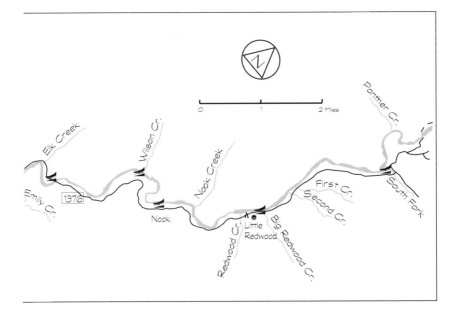

with the spey rod. In high water like this, it was a definite handicap, an ascetic decision akin to wearing a hairshirt while sitting on a bed of nails, but, well, you know how it is when you have a new toy. I just thought about those Sandy River steelhead and persisted with the spey rod.

There's nothing fancy about winter steelheading, regardless of what tackle you use. In essence, you put some kind of lure in front of bottom-hugging fish. If it feels like biting, it will. If it doesn't feel like biting, it won't, and there's little you can do about it. The trick is finding willing fish. Steelhead seek out a certain kind of water, and given a few variables such as water temperature, they will be in that kind of water. The places you find the right water changes with the river level, which will vary greatly with winter conditions. Good winter steelheaders know their home rivers under all conditions and can find fishable water in almost any flow.

That's why I'm not a great winter steelheader. I'm really not even mediocre. The problem is that I'm too peripatetic: I like to see new places, so I don't spend enough time on any one river to know it as well as I should. Then too, I'm always fiddling around with things like spey rods when another tool would have been better equipped to reach the fish.

I moved down to Nook and fished there, again with the spey rod. Several anglers were casting drift gear from the bank but had not hooked any fish. I moved downriver and spied a lone angler where the river made a turn.

"It's looking better," I said as I got near.

"Yep. Might be good tomorrow."

"Any luck?"

"Not yet." He reeled in and got ready for his next cast, but before he tossed it out he said, "What kind of rod is that? I've never seen one like it."

"It's a spey rod, a two-handed fly rod. Fifteen-feet long."

He pointed to a slot about a hundred feet away. "There's some good water just above me. They move through that slower water near the bank, between us and the fast water."

"Are you sure I won't crowd you?"

"No problem. I'd like to see you play a fish on that long rod."

"Me too."

It was a good-looking slot, but the river was still too high and fast. Even casting upstream with my heaviest shooting head, I couldn't feel bottom. I fished the run longer than I should have, mostly out of deference to the other angler's generosity. After half an hour, I moved on.

By noon, I'd tried several runs but had no luck. The river was continuing to drop, though, and I drove to the nearest phone and arranged for a shuttle driver. Shortly after 1:00 I launched the drift-boat at Nook. My plan was to float a section of the river and note the best runs. Then tomorrow, when I drifted it again, I would be familiar with the best places to fish.

It was a pleasant afternoon, rainless and almost warm when the wind stopped. North coast rivers are surrounded by hemlocks and firs, with cedars and alders near the streambeds, but the Chetco's canyon is dressed differently: redwoods, orange-barked madrones, and myrtle. It was a pleasant change of scenery.

I floated from run to run, taking notes on all of them, and fishing every other one. I wasn't serious about my fishing, but I feel you never really get the sense of a steelhead run until you work it over a bit. Some places looked really good, and if the river dropped another foot or two . . . I grinned and shook my head in anticipation of tomorrow's fishing.

When I arrived at the takeout four hours after launching, there was another group of anglers loading their boat onto its trailer.

"Any luck?" I asked.

"Hooked two, lost them both," one of them said.

"Could be good tomorrow," I said.

The guy cranking the winch handle grunted. "Not likely. The radio said there's another storm coming in tonight. A big one."

Back at the motel, I turned on my weather radio. Sure enough, it said the new storm was headed for the coast, and it would hit Brookings between two and six in the morning, twelve hours earlier than they'd previously forecast.

I reasoned it through. If the storm hits around six, then there won't have been enough rain to make the river rise and muddy up. I could still fish, and it will be better than today because it will continue to drop all night.

It was a lie, the kind of angler self-talk that tries to put a good spin on things. The barometer would be dropping, the rain could come before the actual storm, and so on. I could find a lot of reasons why tomorrow would be worse than today. The best fishing in two weeks had been this afternoon; it was unlikely to get better. Once again, I'd been Btfsplk-ed.

The weather radio had another piece of bad news: snow was expected in the coastal mountains by afternoon, and it might extend over the entire state, including Portland. I faced the prospect of 350 miles of snow-covered roads between me and home. I decided to fish until noon, then high-tail it north.

About three in the morning I woke to the sound of rain hammering the motel. It was still pouring when I arrived at the river around seven. The wind wasn't bad, however, so it could have been worse.

I checked out my sticks at Nook. The river was no worse than yesterday, but no better, either. I contemplated launching the boat, then decided not to. If it was going to be stinky weather, I didn't want to be committed to a 12-mile drift, and the possibility of a snowy drive home wasn't attractive either. Better to stay on the bank and get an early start for home.

I donned raingear, assembled the spey rod, and cast my way down the bar. After I'd been casting for two hours, a car pulled onto the bar. A man got out and watched me for a while, then came closer.

"I just got myself one of those spey rods," he said. "I haven't used it yet. Is it hard to learn to cast?"

I gave him my spiel about how it's like learning to cast all over again and showed him a few basics. I offered him the rod, but he declined to try it. I understood; one's first experience with a spey rod should not be in front of strangers.

We talked about the river for a while. The rain had let up, and I even pulled back the hood of my jacket. He told about a bed-and-breakfast place he and his wife were fixing up, then handed me a card and invited me to stay sometime. "Maybe I'll know how to use my spey rod by then, and we can go out and get us some steelhead," he said.

I thanked him and put the card in the pocket of my waders. He left to assemble his drift rod, and I tried a piece of slow water that was overhung with branches. It proved as fruitless as all the other runs.

It was near noon, and my hands were wrinkled and pruny from being in the rain all morning. Although I was warm enough, my shoulders were damp, and I made a note to replace my rain jacket.

Clouds moved through the canyon, and occasionally the sky parted enough to give a glimpse of blue beyond the heavy gray. Maybe in a few days, if the rain stopped, the river would drop and clear. Fresh, mint-bright steelhead would move in, and the fishing would be dynamite. But I had to be in Seattle next week, so some other fortunate soul would experience it. I packed my gear into the truck and headed out. The other angler waved as I left.

When I reached the top of the steep climb to the main road, I had a nice view of the Chetco. It was darker than yesterday's jade green. A shaft of light pierced the cloud layer and made the redwoods and madrones glisten. Then the clouds closed in again.

I should have felt bad. By the time I reached home, I would have been gone five days, driven over a thousand miles, fished under sometimes miserable conditions, tripped in the mud, slid on my butt, almost fallen into an icy river, spent countless hours trying to outsmart fish.

And not one steelhead had given me so much as a half-hearted tap. I hadn't even seen a fish. Not in the river, not on the bank, not at the end of anyone's fishing line. Several people claimed to have hooked steelhead, but no one had brought a fish to the bank. As far as I could tell, all the fish were dead and every angler a liar.

I didn't care.

There had been new rivers and pleasant people, and I'd improved my double spey cast. It wasn't so bad. Some other day I would come back to the Chetco, and the Elk, Sixes, and Coquille. They were not strangers now. I really felt quite satisfied.

I turned the truck onto the main road. About two miles away, a rain squall was moving up the canyon. Soon, it would be over my head. I pointed my face at the dark, ragged cloud and stuck my tongue in my lower lip. I rested my right thumb on my nose, and wriggling my fingers I said, as loud as I could,

"BBBTTTTTFFFFFSSSSSPPPPPLLLLLKKKKK!"

The Restless Season

Early March

An Oregon "winter of our discontent" is not for me. The Northwest is my birthplace, and I was weaned on gray skies and rain. I enjoy the soft, easy-on-the-eyes diffusion of winter light, the way rain moves across the land in ragged curtains, the bending of fir trees to the wind. I actually like an Oregon winter . . . up to a point.

By early March, even a deep-dyed Northwesterner like me is ready for a change, and I grow restless with the approach of spring. After my odyssey to the south coast, I stayed home for a while. I caught up on work, even got ahead. Then the restless feeling rose within me again, and less than two weeks after I returned from the Chetco, I was ready to go somewhere, do something different. I just didn't know what or where.

Steelheading wasn't the answer. I enjoy it, but I wanted a break from big lures, big flies, big rods, and blown-out rivers. I yearned to cast a delicate dry fly, to kick my float tube on a lake, to go to a place that whispered of spring.

Although it was early March, the March browns were not out yet—probably because of the cold, high rivers—so the Valley streams were not an option. The answer lay in the dry country to the east. How far east, I didn't yet know.

I loaded the truck with food, camping gear, rods, float tube, and waders, and turned my back on the coast. I had an invitation to stay at a friend's cabin on the Deschutes, so I would begin there. After that, I had some ideas, but no plans. I'd figure out where I was going when I got there.

Deschutes River near Maupin

There is no month in which an Oregon fly angler cannot go to a river and catch a decent trout on a dry fly. From mid-September through April, the dominant hatches are three almost indistinguishable mayfly genera: *Baetis, Pseudocloeon,* and *Diphetor.*

Most fly anglers lump these insects together and call them blue-winged olives or, sometimes, tiny olives. The more knowledgeable fly fishers call them Baetis, although that properly identifies only one of the three genera, albeit the most common.

Nearly all of the *Baetis* cognoscenti pronounce the word "BAIT-us", as in "bait us up with another of them worms." I pronounce it "BEET-us." The professional entomologists I know (all two of them) say it that way, and I know two hot-shot, world-class angler/writers who use BEET-us. (To be honest, that's actually only three people because one of the angler/writers is also one of the entomologists.)

I once asked a woman who had studied for a Ph.D. in classical languages which was right, BAIT-us or BEET-us. She said that first of all she'd studied more Greek than Latin and shouldn't render an opinion, but if I was really interested (I was), there were scientific Latin, church Latin, French Latin, and probably a few more I forget, and they do not agree on the proper pronunciation of the a-e dipthong. As far as she was concerned, neither BAIT-us nor BEET-us is correct, but BEET-us is closer to right. So I stick with BEET-us.

This gets me into trouble unless I'm talking to the one-and-a-half professional entomologists or the one-and-a-half hot-shot angler/writers. When I say BEET-us to someone I don't know, they act embarrassed and look at their shoes, as if I'd just scratched my genitals while on a public stage. Yet I can tell the difference between a *Baetis*, a *Pseudocloeon*, and a *Diphetor*, which I bet is more than they can do. Further, they never actually say anything, thus denying me an opportunity to engage in pedantic enlightenment and explain that if they're going to say BAIT-us, then for consistency they should also refer to the great Roman general as Hulius KAY-sar (not Julius CEE-ser), a man they can look up in the encyclo-PAY-dia (not encyclo-PEE-dia).

The world of fly fishing abounds in quiet controversies like BAIT-us and BEET-us, and some people take them pretty seriously. All I've learned from the *Baetis* thing is that it doesn't always pay to be right, and that there are a lot of fly fishers, including me, who need to get a life.

Trout, on the other hand, know no linguistic controversies and simply call these insects "lunch." Fall and winter, they are the most important bug in the river. Winter hatches usually begin between 1:00 and 2:00 most afternoons. The insects are ubiquitous; I've never been on a river that didn't have at least a few of them. December and January are sometimes a bit lean, but late February through March the hatches can be prolific.

Any stream that supports a healthy trout population can provide good winter *Baetis* fishing. Two of the best are the Deschutes and the Crooked. How good can it be? A couple of years ago I was walking along the Deschutes above the Locked Gate (south of

Maupin) and saw the flash of feeding trout in a backeddy. I tied on a size 18 Comparadun, and in the next hour I landed over a dozen trout, each one a bright fish between 15 and 18 inches. That's not bad dry fly fishing for a day in late February. If you fish the Deschutes much, you'll realize that means I spent far more time playing trout than casting to them. I felt satisfied even after I discovered my car battery was dead and I was six miles from town.

Some days, however, the *Baetis* are no-shows, or the hatch never gathers momentum. The best days are cool and overcast or, better yet, drizzly. Cold, damp weather seems to bring out more insects, and it keeps the duns on the water longer. Trout key on the drifting duns, especially in backeddies and slow runs, and when it's good, it's very good indeed.

The duns are not the only important stage of the insect. They come back to lay their eggs (this stage is called the "spinner"), but most fly anglers neither recognize this nor fish it any better than they pronounce *Baetis*. Most mayflies sprawl on the surface to lay eggs, or drop them from above, but *Baetis* swim below the surface to lay theirs. This is one reason a wet fly can be a good pattern during a Baetis hatch. I believe many trout—especially the bigger ones—prefer to take their Baetis underwater.

The nymphs are also important. They drift in the current near the river bottom, and a size 18 Pheasant Tail or Gold-Ribbed Hares Ear (use dark brown fur) dead-drifted along the gravel can provide action throughout the day. Most of that action will not come from trout, however. In the Deschutes, whitefish are more active in winter than trout (they are more tolerant of cold water) and outnumber the trout by at least five to one.

When I'm looking for a little winter action and the trout aren't sipping duns, I tie on a heavy stonefly nymph, then put a small nymph on a dropper 8-12 inches above it. The stone nymph is there for weight; it gets the small nymph near the bottom. You could do the same thing with a split shot, but I find a stone nymph/dropper rig easier to cast and more productive.

I drift this rig through slow runs, in slow water next to fast water, and in other places where food and whitefish might collect.

Because whitefish tend to school up, once you find one you've found dozens, and you can wear your arm out nymphing to them in winter.

Jim Colthurst slid his blue Geo Spectrum to a stop at the pull-out a few miles below Sherars Bridge on the Deschutes. We'd had a leisurely breakfast at his cabin in Maupin and were just getting started even though it was near 11:00. That's one of the great things about fishing the *Baetis* hatch: you can sleep in.

Jim got out of the car and surveyed the gray skies. "I hope we get some rain," he said. Jim is a good angler and fishes the Deschutes a lot. He knew as well as anyone that a little rain improves this hatch. The day before, we'd fished in sunshine and it was a slow go, so we were glad to see overcast skies. Oregon anglers pray for rain more often than you want to know.

We donned waders, then raingear (at this point, the latter was more hopeful than necessary) and walked to the river. Jim began working the middle section of the run with a dry fly, while I went to the riffle that begins the run. Below the riffle the river flowed at a good clip, but there was a patch of slow water between the fast water and the rock I stood on. Bubbles of foam revealed the pace and direction of the current.

Unlike Jim, I was using nymphs in my standard winter rigging: a Pheasant Tail dropper with a heavy Girdlebug on the point. My cast was short—about 10 feet of line past the rod tip—and I mended so the line was upstream from where the fly entered the water. The mend lets the nymphs sink quickly. I lifted the rod as the rig came back to me and heard a "tick" (I "hear" it through the finger that holds the line to the cork grip; I have no explanation for why it feels audible). I jerked the rod up a foot. Meeting no resistance, I lowered it again. A few seconds later there was another tick and the leader stopped moving. I lifted the rod and it pulled back.

The fish ran downstream and yanked ten feet of line off the reel, then came in with token resistance. It was what I expected. Whitefish are not strong swimmers and poop-out quickly. I brought the fish to my hand, worked the tiny nymph out of its small mouth, and released it.

I continued casting until I had landed eight or ten fish, then moved downstream a few hundred yards and worked the current seams through a boulder-strewn area where I caught some more. At half-past noon, I returned to where Jim was casting his dry flies.

"How'd you do," he asked.

"A dozen and a half fish, or so," I said. "How about you?"

"I had three. Mine were trout."

"One of mine was a trout," I said.

Jim closed his eyes and shook his head. Most Deschutes anglers view whitefish as a poor consolation prize for not catching a trout.

We ate a riverside lunch and waited for the hatch to begin. Although it was humid, rain never quite materialized, and we knew it would be a so-so hatch, if it happened at all. A little after one o'clock, Jim said, "There's one." We watched the dun float down the river, flutter its wings, then lift off. Another one floated by and flew away, then one disappeared in a swirl of water.

Jim put his sandwich down. "We can eat later," he said, reaching for his rod.

I already had mine in my hand and had exchanged the nymph rig for a dry fly. We stood about a hundred feet apart and cast to rising fish, hooking fewer than we felt we deserved, but still having fun. About an hour after the first dun was sucked into a trout's mouth, the hatch began to fade. I let my dry fly dangle in the water fifty feet below me while I looked for more rises upstream. The rod almost jerked out of my hand, and the line zinged toward mid-river. A fat trout, easily 16-inches long, cleared the water and fell back with a splash, snapping my tippet.

I looked at Jim. "It was fun while it lasted," I said, "but it could have lasted longer."

It was the final fling of the hatch. We kept casting, but there were no decent fish who were interested. Jim finally said, "Let's move on. I know a place we can pick up some fish." He looked at me sternly. "I mean trout."

"Sure," I said. "Just give me a minute." I was putting the nymph rig back together. "Be with you in a sec."

Jim rolled his eyes. "OK," he said. "But not more than a half dozen whitefish."

Crooked River below Bowman Dam

Some old timers claim the Crooked River used to have the best trout fishing in Oregon, much better than the Deschutes. I can believe it. Not many years ago the Crooked was dam-free and flowed directly into the Deschutes. Now Bowman Dam blocks the river just east of Prineville, and the Round Butte/Pelton project backs up the Deschutes, Metolius, and Crooked rivers near Warm Springs. Further, the summer water levels in the Crooked are changed frequently to meet the needs of irrigators. These fluctuations inhibit the growth of aquatic insects and other critters that trout grow big on.

The river's still pretty good, however.

Like the Deschutes, the Crooked has cut a spectacular canyon through the basalt flows of central Oregon. A paved road parallels the river from near Prineville to Bowman Dam. The last few miles before the dam have several BLM-administered recreation sites set among the sage and juniper.

The Crooked is popular with winter fly fishers who come to fish the *Baetis* hatch and the scuds. Scuds are crustaceans that thrive in slow, weedy water. Although they rarely exceed half-an-inch in length, they are prolific and make trout fat and sassy. On the Crooked in winter, trout prefer orange-tinted scud patterns.

The typical Crooked River rainbow is about 12-inches long. There are bigger fish, as well as smaller, and there are a lot of them. It's not the same as the Deschutes, but it's good enough and a nice change. In my restless mood, variety was what I sought, so after two days on the Deschutes with Jim Colthurst, I headed for the Crooked.

I found it as muddy as any stream I'd encountered in this muddy-river winter. When I stuck my rod tip into the water to check the turbidity, I couldn't see more than an inch.

Nevertheless, at 1:00 the *Baetis* began hatching, and trout rose to take them. I stationed myself beside a run where the river passed through a boulder field. Foam lines indicated where the current was concentrated. I'm a big believer in casting to foam lines because the same current that concentrates foam will concentrate food, and therefore trout. I cast my dry fly into a line of bubbles and was instantly rewarded with a hookup.

The trout was five-inches long. I'm not one of those anglers who searches only for "hawgs," but I admit that I prefer my trout to be a foot long or better. While the Crooked offers fewer fish of that size than the Deschutes, this fish was small even by the diminished standards of the river.

I released the rainbow and continued casting. More fish took my fly, and in short order I landed and released a half dozen or more. All were between five and seven inches.

This puzzled me. I knew the river held bigger fish, but where were they? Was I on a small-fish stretch of river? Not likely. The run was over three-feet deep and had sufficient cover to support larger trout.

I clipped off the dry fly and switched to my Girdlebug-and-Pheasant Tail rig. I cast it into the run. It drifted only a couple of feet before stopping, and I tightened on a fish. This one had more heft to it, and soon I was releasing a 12-incher. I continued to cast into the run and hooked a half dozen more trout before they got wise to me. Every fish was between 10 and 13 inches, double the size of those that had taken my dry fly, yet from the same water.

Each of those trout took the size 18 Pheasant Tail nymph, a fly that's less than a quarter of an inch long. All of them took it near the bottom in muddy water over three-feet deep. The amount of light reaching those trout would have been indiscernible to a human eye, and there had to be a lot of nymph-sized debris drifting through. Yet they consistently picked out my tiny, dark brown fly.

Think about that the next time you think you need a big, flashy lure to "get the fish's attention."

Chickahominy Reservoir

The Crooked River was fun, but the restless mood hadn't faded much. It had been almost five months since I'd fished a lake, and I was missing stillwater. Oregon's desert lakes are the best places to find trout this early in the year, and one of the lakes that turns on first is Chickahominy Reservoir. I was there by 3:30.

"There" is a mudhole in the middle of nowhere, surrounded by nothing. Made by man to serve the needs of irrigators, Chickahominy lies just off US 26 east of Hampton, west of Riley, and north of Wagontire—all communities that support a gas station, at most.

Despite its status as a shoe-in for a "most ugly fishing lake" contest, Chickahominy has one redeeming beauty: big rainbow trout. As in most Northwest desert lakes, fish grow fast here.

The reservoir squats in a depression in the sagebrush plains. Some hills lie to the north, but otherwise there's not much to stop the wind, which was blowing about 20 mph out of a gray 42-degree sky when I arrived. A few boats were on the lake. Fishing rods were held stiffly by raw, red hands. Anglers were bundled in parkas and hoods and sat with hunched shoulders. I suspect they were all thinking the same thing: "Can we quit yet?"

I drove around the lake looking for a good place to camp. While the gravel road that leads to Chickahominy is in good shape, and the boat ramp is easily reached, access to the rest of the lake can be tricky. The roads (dirt trails, really) are rutted and rough, and recent rains had turned them into a slippery goo. I shifted into four-wheel drive and hoped it would be enough.

On the lake's west side, I found a place where the wind would be at my back, thus making it easier and less dangerous to cast from shore. As soon as I was set up, the wind shifted and blew in my face.

No problem. I'd fish from the float tube. I donned my expedition-weight capilene long-johns and a thick pair of socks, then covered both socks and underwear with neoprene waders and slipped on neoprene booties. My torso was clad in two capilene turtlenecks, a polar fleece jacket, and a rain jacket (the latter more to block the wind than the wet). I put on my wool hat and launched the float tube.

I was freezing within ten minutes.

A check of the water temperature revealed the reason: it was 42 degrees, same as the air. It wasn't bad when the sun came out and the wind stopped, but those blessed events didn't happen often. It was near 4:00 when I began fishing. I set the alarm on my watch to 5:30 and promised my body we'd quit when the alarm went off.

I rigged up with an olive Woolly Bugger on an intermediate sinking line and kicked slowly along the shore. Chickahominy's visibility was little better than the Crooked River's. The lake is always that way because the wind stirs it up so much.

I neared a couple of old guys sitting on folding chairs on the bank, their rods propped on sticks. I changed course to avoid their lines.

"Any luck?" I asked as I passed.

"Not today," one of them said. "We did good yesterday, though."

We talked back and forth for a while. Then one of them said, "Uh-oh. I think that's a bite." He picked up his rod, waited a space, then jerked back.

"Damn," he said. "Missed him."

His friend looked at his watch. "Must be time for the 4:25 bite," he joked. "We'd better hang on tight."

I chuckled, but was cut short when my rod jumped. There was no hookup, however. I turned around, trolled past the same area, and had another fishy grab that missed the hook.

After forty minutes in the water, my extremities were thoroughly chilled. I headed for shore and walked around until they started to feel normal again, then went out and tubed some more. A check of my watch showed it was almost 5:00. *Oh good*, I thought. *I only have to do this another thirty minutes.*

Then a fish hit, this time solidly hooking itself. The trout ran straight at me, and even though I hauled line frantically and backpedaled as fast as I could, it was hard to keep the line tight. Ten feet from the tube, the rainbow jumped. My jaw dropped. This trout was the size of a small steelhead.

It turned and ran from me until it was well into my backing, then jumped again. After the two jumps and hard runs it became more docile, and I was soon working the hook out of the mouth of a fat, four-pound rainbow. I released it and went looking for another.

Five minutes later my rod jumped again, and I was onto a trout that could have been twin to the first. I landed this fish, too, and released it.

I was surprised at how warm I now felt. My toes were no longer numb, and when my watch alarm beeped at 5:30, I turned it off and kept fishing. I quit for dinner around dark.

The truck rocked in the wind as I slept in it that night. I awoke to sunshine flooding in beneath a layer of dark clouds. The sun warmed the truck's interior, and I dozed through the early morning in my down sleeping bag. Getting up didn't seem very important.

Eventually I got hungry, however, and climbed out to greet the morning. The day was much the same as its predecessor, except now the northern hills had a skim of snow about 200 feet higher than Chickahominy.

I dressed even warmer than the day before, and kicked the tube around my end of the lake with the same olive Woolly Bugger I'd used yesterday (it's a tough fly to beat in any lake). I had five grabs, but no fish. By 11:00, I was packed and on the road again, the winter restlessness sitting squarely between my shoulder blades.

Owyhee River

In 1819, an exploration party in eastern Oregon tangled with Indians. Two members of the party—natives of the Sandwich Islands—were killed, and a nearby river was given the name of their homeland. They called it "Owyhee," the aboriginal name for the Sandwich Islands. Today, we call those islands Hawaii, but Owyhee stuck for this Oregon river.

There are two Owyhee rivers in Oregon, or rather one stream with two very different characters. Above Owyhee Reservoir, the river is remote and rugged. Favored by whitewater boaters for its stunning canyons and tough rapids, it supports a productive small-mouth bass fishery. Below the dam that creates the lake, the Owyhee River is slow-moving, almost stagnant in many places. In summer, it is drawn down for irrigation and becomes too warm for good fishing, but in spring and fall it offers excellent opportunities for catching rainbows and brown trout.

The restless spirit that took me first to the Deschutes, then to the Crooked and on to Chickahominy, dropped me here. On the way, I'd stopped at the Malheur River and found it too high and muddy for fishing. I'd thought about Mann Lake and decided it would be too windy, so I kept driving until I reached the Owyhee, hard by the Idaho border.

It was late afternoon when I arrived. I pulled over at a more-or-less randomly-selected spot and scanned the river. Trout were rising in a rocky, slow-moving pool below me, so I climbed into my waders, grabbed a rod, and went for a closer look.

I couldn't see what they were rising to, but the rod I took down was one I'd used on the Deschutes, and a *Baetis* Comparadun was still tied to the tippet. It looked as likely to catch a fish as any fly in my box, so I cast it out. The Comparadun drifted three feet before a trout sucked it down. I tightened, the rod quivered, and I soon was releasing a fat 11-inch rainbow.

Eight or ten more followed as I worked upstream through the pool. All were between 10 and 15 inches. One of the fish had fresh wounds on its back, and I looked around to see if there were any eagles or osprey in the canyon.

When I reached the end of the good water, I crossed the river and walked upstream to the next pool. A couple of anglers were fishing it with worms. One had a 20-inch rainbow on a stringer, and the other said he'd hooked and released a brown trout of about five pounds (all the Owyhee's browns must be released unharmed, a hard thing to do when bait is allowed).

I switched to a streamer and worked some of the deeper pools for brown trout, but had no luck. By evening, I headed for the border town of Ontario in search of a motel bed and shower. An owl swooped through my headlights as I drove out.

The next morning I was on the river shortly after sunup. I should have been there earlier, but the motel bed just felt too good to surrender. My quarry for the day was brown trout. Forget the rainbows; I'd gone the entire season without a trophy-sized brown, and I wanted one. The basalt-bound pool I picked was sure to have at least one.

In fact, it held more than one. When I arrived, two big fish were rising at the head of the pool. A weak current brought an occasional, light-colored mayfly into their feeding lane, and each mayfly went down with a slurp. I cast over the browns for a while and had a couple of refusals, but I just didn't have the right fly in my box.

Farther down the pool, where the water was lake-like, there was a huge splash. I bid farewell to the two risers and went for a look. After I'd sat on the bank a while, there was another splash. It wasn't the sort of commotion a rising trout makes, nor was it from a jump. It came from a big brown trout slashing through a school of smaller fish.

My fingers trembled as I tied on a streamer. I worked it through the pool as best I knew how, but the only result was that the brown trout stopped feeding near the surface.

The Owyhee is a shallow river, slow-moving and turbid. It gurgles through shallow, bouldery riffles, then broadens into pools that can be surprisingly deep. A little after noon, I was sitting on the cooler eating lunch beside one of these pools.

On the other side of the river, the canyon wall rose straight up several hundred feet. The walls here have a red tinge, not the brown and yellow hues of the Deschutes and Crooked canyons. Wind and river had eroded the rock into fantastic, tortured shapes—spires, chimneys, and caves were everywhere.

It was a warm day, near sixty, and white clouds dotted a deep blue sky. Wind rustled in the grass, ruffled the pages of the book I held, made the power lines hum an eerie tune. I heard the skree of an eagle, the woosh of a merganser flock, the skronk of geese, the coo of doves.

At first I wished I knew more about birds and rocks, but the feeling faded and I tried to appreciate it for what it was and not examine it through the tunnel vision of some "ology." As I did so, my restless feeling began to ebb. I was content to just sit in the warming day and let the canyon wash over me.

I'd have contemplated it all longer, but I heard a trout rise in the pool. Rod and tackle bag in hand, I headed to the river.

The pool's surface was dotted with several rises. There were not a lot of them, but enough to suggest active feeding by a half dozen or more trout. I couldn't see what they were taking, but there were a few midges on the surface and some mayflies. I knew from this morning that the trout didn't like the mayflies I was chucking at them, so I tried various midge patterns.

Unlike yesterday, when rainbow trout gobbled my flies with gay abandon, I was having a tough time getting any respect from these fish. From that—and the slow water they were in—I concluded they were brown trout. After an hour of fruitless fishing and many changes of fly, I finally caught a fish on a small, tan midge pupa I pulled slowly through the pool. It was a brown trout, fat and about 18 inches long. I figured I had their number now, and repeated the presentation and fly that had brought me this single success.

I might as well have cast a fly-less leader for all the attention the trout paid me.

An otter family undulated along the opposite bank, and I suspected they had a den over there. No wonder the fish were wary. Suddenly, water erupted in the middle of the pool. Undoubtedly one of the otters had taken a fish. I looked for a bewhiskered head to pop up, but saw none. Again, water sprayed all over, and a big bow wave rolled across the pool.

This was no otter; this was a trophy brown trout attacking

smaller trout. It was a fish big enough that the otters should worry about *it*.

I switched to a streamer and cast to this Big Kahuna of the Owyhee. No luck. I went through my black leeches, brown leeches, Matukas, sculpins, dry flies, and wet flies. I presented upstream, downstream, across stream. I tried floating lines, sinking lines, thick leaders, and thin leaders. I tried other pools, then returned. I rested the water for an hour. On every cast I expected the sudden, hard pull of a big trout. I reaped only water and weeds.

The blue flame of the stove reflected off the truck as I stirred my freeze-dried Tuna Alfredro. I ate it sitting on the cooler and listened to the wind in the dark canyon. I hadn't heard a car for twenty minutes, so I was probably the only person left in this wild place. A rock broke loose and clattered down the canyon's face. How many such rocks does it take to make a place like this? Geese honked downstream. It's a mystery to me why geese can't be quiet at night.

Every ten minutes or so I heard a big splash. The big brown was working the pool again, but I'd given up on it. I had fished until dark and finally wove fly line and leader into a hopeless tangle that only daylight could straighten out.

Almost a year ago, I'd set off in pursuit of a trophy brown trout. I'd caught a few nice browns, but the most memorable fish was probably an illusion. Still, it had been a good year. I'd had my chinook on the Willamette and, as a reward for self-righteous perseverance, there had been a superb day of trophy rainbows on Crane Prairie. I'd had my spring-time visit to Mecca Flat, and companionable floats down the Deschutes and John Day. I'd learned to use a spey rod, and had some winter steelhead with it. There had been cutthroat and sturgeon, bass and kokanee, high lakes and tidewater, ocean and desert.

On the Owyhee, the signs of spring were clear: budding willows, returning birds, active fish, warming air. The circle of the endless season was almost complete. The earth had already returned to the same point in its orbit as when Maddy Sheehan and I had fished the McKenzie. Yet I did not count the cycle as finished because I hadn't seen a March brown yet. Soon enough, one would drift on the surface of an Oregon river. An irridescent trout would sip it down, and once more I'd be at an end that is also a beginning.

Overhead, the dipper hung in the northern sky, Orion in the east. The half moon blurred through a gathering haze. A few doves called softly from the cliffs across the Owyhee. My restless feeling had evaporated. I felt peace and contentment in the canyon's solitude, but I was ready for people again. Tomorrow I'd be on the Interstate, not the river. It was time for home and family.

There was splash in the river—Big Kahuna, mocking my inadequacy. I shook my head and laughed. Somewhere in the canyon, a coyote answered.

21

Urban Paranoia

Mid-March, Clackamas River below Barton

I haven't been arrested yet, but I'm sure someday soon there'll be a county sheriff waiting for me at the Carver boat ramp. He'll tell me to put my big rod down—"real slow now"—cuff my hands behind my back, and push me into his patrol car.

It's the guys in jet boats, the ones who fish the Clackamas in winter; they want me off their river. They've probably already told their legislator to draft a new felony law: "fishing from an inferior watercraft." Then they'll nail me.

Although the Clack's hatchery salmon and steelhead runs have declined, there's no shortage of moneyed fishermen. You used to see a lot of driftboats here, but the last few years their numbers have dwindled, and jet boats dominate the river. I take this as a bad sign: if you can't impress somebody with your catch, you dazzle them with a fancy toy.

I don't have anything against wealthy anglers, or even against jet boats. Some decent folks own them, including friends of mine. But the Clack attracts the worst of the bunch, real power anglers who think nothing of paying $25,000 for boats with brand names like "Predator."

It's not the boats I object to. It's the arrogance. These guys roar up and down the river wearing sunglasses, hard grins, and camouflage jackets. Camouflage—what a joke. The only place they could blend in would be a drag strip.

I'm sure it's my imagination, but every time I drift the Clackamas it seems like I'm the only one on the river without a motor. Even the McKenzie boats all seem to have an eight-horse Mercury on the transom.

I once met a guy who claims he fishes the Clackamas from a 12-foot cataraft, but I've never seen him there. I think he fishes the Sandy now, on the section where jet boats are banned.

It's not just my motorless boat that makes me slightly paranoid on the Clackamas. It's my spey rod, too. Fly fishers are rare enough on the river, but when I started taking my 15-foot two-hander, I became an oddity among eccentrics.

After my return from the Owyhee, I was content to stay closer to home, which meant half-day trips to the Clackamas. Unlike the Sandy's wild feeling, the lower Clackamas—from Barton Park to the mouth—has a suburban ambiance. You're never far from a house or people. Still, it's a nice trip. There is enough wildlife to make me feel like I'm out of the city, if not in the wilderness, and a few fish still swim in the river.

The Clackamas supports both spring and fall chinook, as well as winter and summer steelhead. Most of the fish come from hatcheries, but in late winter a run of wild steelhead surges upstream in search of spawning gravel. Some of these fish are a hefty fifteen pounds or more.

The second week of March, I was on the Clackamas looking for those fish. The spey rod was still new enough that I didn't want to give it up, so I persisted with it, even though a spinner or drift rig would have yielded more fish.

It was Friday, and I was making my third drift of the week, searching for runs suitable for the spey rod. The river was a bit high, but it was dropping and had that jade color favored by steelheaders. Bright green buds dotted the willow stems, and flocks of Canada geese flew past. Geese honk a lot when they fly. They're like the jet boat guys: they can't go anywhere without making noise. I don't mind the geese.

I stopped at one spot, parking my driftboat along the bank upstream from the run. I walked down and checked it out. It looked too fast, but I wondered if it would be fishable if the river dropped another half-foot or so. I waded in and took a few casts anyway, just to see how the current twisted.

I was into my fourth cast when a big jet boat came around the bend like thunder across the prairie. The guy throttled back as he went by me. He looked at my rod and gave me a cocky smile (he'd already passed my boat). Then he pointed at the water and said, "Ya think that's going to hold the big one today?" He had that tone of voice people use when they describe their neighbor's religion.

After he passed me, he revved up the engine—a few rpm more than necessary, I thought—and accelerated around the next bend. The noise faded until all I could hear was the river hissing against my legs. I knew what that jet boater was saying to himself: "Har, har, har. Couldn't afford a *real* boat." Followed by a sneering, "*Dickhead.*"

Two runs later I was alone and fishing a good stretch of water. My fly hung up in mid-river. Rock or fish? I swung the rod toward shore and felt a throbbing resistance. In the river, I saw a broad flash of silver. Ten minutes later I had the steelhead on the bank, a wild hen of about seven pounds. Not as big as those wild March fish can be, but respectable.

Before releasing her, my ears sifted the sounds of the river. They found nothing but wind and an occasional goose. I strained for what I longed to hear. The fish would be OK; she was resting in the water, and if I held her up for a few seconds to show her off, it wouldn't hurt. But the air was empty of unnatural sounds.

There's never a jet boat around when you want one.

I continued to drift my way to the takeout at Carver. I passed an alder that was starting to leaf out. It was a precocious tree, a week or two ahead of its siblings, who showed a yellow-green fuzz against the blue and white sky. The willows were nearly ready to put out their leaves. Many of the stems had been nibbled by beavers, and the short, beveled stubs angled out about ankle-high, ready to poke holes in the waders of the unwary. Spring was coming here, as surely as I'd seen it on the Owyhee. But the one sign I sought was absent: there were no March browns.

In my previous two trips this week, I'd seen afternoon hatches that brought trout to the surface, but they were tiny *Baetis*, not the big March browns. So when I came around a bend at 1:30 and saw rising trout, I paid little attention. Even when I saw mayflies lifting from the river, it took a few minutes before it registered: these bugs were not tiny, they were big; they were not olive, they were brown.

Recognition dawned, and I rowed into a backeddy to watch the trout sip the duns. I didn't have a trout rod with me, but that didn't matter. After ten minutes, I pulled for shore and got out. The spey rod stayed in the boat, and I quick-stepped to the head of a small riffle on the back side of an island. Rolling my sleeves up, I plunged my hands into the water up to my elbows and picked up a rock. Flat, dark brown nymphs scurried away on the back side as it came out of the water. I picked up a nymph and examined it, pushing my glasses up and bringing it within three inches of my nearsighted eyes. It was a March brown, and down its back, between the shoulders, was a thin white line. It was ready to hatch. Maybe not today, but tomorrow or the next day.

The circle was complete.

Epilogue

Several events have happened in the months since I made the fishing trips described in this book. First, steps are being taken to protect coastal cutthroat trout (Chapter 8), but only after the cutthroats in the Umpqua River drainage were declared an endangered species. I only hope it's not too late.

Also, the Oregon Fish and Wildlife Commission decided to decrease the upper size limit on sturgeon (Chapter 6) to 60 inches so more fish will contribute to natural spawning; now if they'd raise the minimum size to 48 inches, we'd have a slot that started to make sense.

The damselfly migration at Crane Prairie Reservoir (Chapter 7) was just as big a bust the next July as it was when I went there. The reasons remain unclear, but theories abound. The good news (for me) is that nobody's played tapes of Elvis near my tent for the past year.

Martin James returned to the Deschutes River a year after the trip recorded in Chapter 15. While drifting a Green Butt Skunk through the Crow's Nest run below Beavertail, he hooked and landed a feisty six-pound steelhead. He wore a grin as big as the drift boat for the rest of the day and kept saying, "Coor, that fish pulled my string!"